Indi

Your Guide to Ma...
is an essential resource for publishers and authors!

"Sarah Bolme has done a tremendous service for small Christian publishers and their authors by compiling and writing *Your Guide to Marketing Books in the Christian Marketplace*. The numbers of new Christian books published each year is huge; the competition is ferocious; and success for the small Christian publisher depends upon being able to access all available resources. The knowledge Sarah shares is important if one is to succeed in Christian book-publishing today. I recommend her book as a must-read for every Christian author and publisher."

Louis Moore, Publisher
Hannibal Books
www.hannibalbooks.com

"This guide is a must-have resource for every Christian author and publisher."

Linda Evans Shepherd, Founder
Advanced Writers & Speakers Association
www.awsawomen.org

"Sarah removes the scariness of the unknown and replaces it with the specific knowledge you need to market your book for the Christian audience, and the encouragement to persevere. She not only provides resource listings with specific contact information, but explains the resources for newcomers to the Christian marketplace.

"Bethany Press - Custom Solutions is excited to have this valuable resource for our customers! We believe that it will provide them with the practical information they need to succeed."

Sara Needham
Bethany Press - Custom Solutions
www.bethanypress.com

"As one of the largest distributors of Christian books, we see that the most common cause of books not doing well is the lack of good marketing. Sarah's book does a great job of guiding authors and publishers in making sure they build consumer and trade awareness and demand for their book."

Larry Carpenter, General Manager
FaithWorks
www.faithworksonline.com

"*Your Guide to Marketing Books in the Christian Marketplace* is well organized."

Linda Jewell, Executive Director
CLASServices, Inc.
www.classervices.com

your guide to
MARKETING
books in the
Christian marketplace

sarah bolme

Crest Publications
Charlotte, NC

Your Guide to Marketing Books in the Christian Marketplace
Copyright © 2006 by Sarah Bolme.

All rights reserved. No part of this book may be reproduced or transmitted in any form or by any means, electronic or mechanical, including photocopying, recording, or saved on any information storage and retrieval system, without permission in writing from the publisher.

All scripture quotations are taken from the Holy Bible New International Version® NIV®, Copyright © 1973, 1978, 1984 by International Bible Society. Used with permission.

ISBN-13: 978-0-9725546-5-7
ISBN-10: 0-9725546-5-3

Library of Congress Control Number: 2006903566

Printed in the United States of America
First Edition: 2006

CREST Publications and the shield logo are trademarks of CREST Publications.

Cover design: Tonya Clarkston
Cover photograph: Sami Sarkis

Published by:
CREST Publications
P.O. Box 481022
Charlotte, NC 28269
www.crestpub.com
www.marketingchristianbooks.com

*To my wonderful husband, Edward;
without his loving support and encouragement
this book would not exist.*

Table of Contents

Foreword 1
Introduction 3

Section I: Launching Your Books
1: Get Connected 7
2: Secure Distribution 21
3: Announce Your Books 29
4: Garner Book Reviews 37
5: Pursue Book Awards 55

Section II: Selling Your Books
6: Reach Christian Retail Stores 65
7: Connect with Churches 89
8: Access Christian Consumers 101
9: Harness the Internet 131
10: Handle Overstocks and Remainders 149

Section III: Special Markets
11: The Christian Homeschool Market 157
12: eBooks 175
13: Spanish Language Books 183

Foreword

I HEAR FROM NEW BOOK AUTHORS all the time whose typical lament is: "I have a book coming out—or my book has come out—but I have no idea what to do to get it out into the marketplace." I'm always looking for good resources to help, and since I deal almost exclusively with Christian authors, I want those resources to reflect the unique needs of that market.

I can't tell you how delighted I was to find *Your Guide to Marketing Books in the Christian Marketplace*. It is not only full of great helps and practical ideas for marketing your own book; it is also a wealth of Christian-oriented resources. Since the job of marketing needs to start long before the book is released, this book will be most helpful to those who are market savvy enough to start the process as soon as the contract is signed. However, if you didn't get started as soon as you should have, you will still find a lot of resources to help you make up for the lost time.

One of the best features of this guide is that it takes you step-by-step through the various aspects of promotion—not just telling you what you should do, but how to find the contacts that will be critical to your success. The listings of organizations, reviewers, consumer groups, and websites alone are worth the price of the book.

I would encourage writers to read through the book first to become aware of all the possibilities for promoting their book, then go back and work through each section applying what looks like it will work for promoting their particular book. It's the application of these tricks of the trade that will make the difference between successful sales and a garage full of unsold books.

One thing that shines through as you read this book is the author's knowledge of the industry. Sarah Bolme has written a book to fill an ongoing need in the industry, based on her years of experience working with authors and small publishers. It's obvious that she's also done her homework to bring you up-to-date resources to make your job easier. You can trust the author and follow the path she has laid out with confidence.

Now, with this tool in hand, you're prepared to launch out into the exciting job that lies ahead.

Sally E. Stuart
Christian Writers' Market Guide
www.stuartmarket.com

Introduction 0

*We will shout for joy when you are victorious
and will lift up our banners in the name of our God.
May the Lord grant all your requests.*

—*Psalm 20:5*

As the director of Christian Small Publishers Association (CSPA), I receive many inquiries about marketing and selling books in the Christian marketplace. I have found that the knowledge base both of marketing techniques and of the Christian marketplace varies widely from inquirer to inquirer. I decided to write this book not as a substitute for all the superb books on book marketing already available, but as a supplement to provide an overall view of the Christian marketplace and to equip publishers, self-publishers, and authors alike with specific resource names and contact information for marketing your books in this niche marketplace.

The Christian marketplace is unique. Knowledge is essential to success in reaching this market. Christian retailers and Christian consumers are inundated with Christian products. Many rely heavily on publisher or author name recognition when making purchasing decisions. Marketing research shows that consumers need to see a new product multiple times before they decide to purchase. For newcomers in the Christian marketplace, knowledge and perseverance are your keys to success.

The three most common mistakes I see new publishers and authors make are:
1. not acquiring the information needed to reach the Christian marketplace effectively,
2. not acquiring distribution for the Christian marketplace, and
3. giving up too soon.

Marketing and selling books is not a sprint; it is a marathon. Especially for newcomers in the Christian marketplace, establishing oneself as a viable resource of quality Christian materials takes time. Many small and self-publishers do experience success in the Christian marketplace through perseverance and a comprehensive marketing strategy.

If you have pondered whether your publishing company should enter the realm of religious books, you will be delighted to hear that this category of books is selling well. Religious book sales have been growing faster than overall book sales.

I pray that this book will be a valuable resource to you as you strive to bring new insights and inspiration to the family of God. May God bless you and the books that He leads you to produce to encourage, teach, and equip His people.

His servant,
Sarah Bolme

P.S.: Correspondence from readers is welcome—just email me at info@marketingchristianbooks.com.

Section I

Launching Your Books

Get Connected   1

Plans fail for lack of counsel, but with many advisers they succeed.
—*Proverbs 15:22*

THE INDUSTRY OF PUBLISHING and bookselling is in constant motion. What is true today for this business will not necessarily be true next year. Knowledge is vital for success in the publishing and bookselling trade. Publishers and authors must strive to stay abreast of industry happenings and trends. Knowing your competition and what they are doing is smart business. Understanding the current trends of Christian retail stores and Christian consumers allows you to market your products wisely. The best way to gather the information required to stay up-to-date about this industry is to get connected.

Join a Publishers Association

Name recognition is an essential ingredient in marketing your book in the Christian marketplace. With the myriad of Christian books available today, Christian retailers are inundated with product choices and do not have the time to screen every book they stock in their stores. As a result, most Christian retailers rely on name recognition to ensure that the products they carry contain messages that are consistent with Protestant or Catholic Christian views and are not other religious materials dressed up in Christian attire.

Christian retailers tend to rely on five main sources for name recognition in considering materials for their stores:

- Known Christian author or personality
- Established Christian publishing house
- Endorsement by a known Christian personality
- Favorable review by a reputable Christian source
- Alliance with a Christian publishers association

Since new small and self-publishers are not established Christian publishing houses and typically are not publishing titles by established Christian personalities, pursuing the other three choices are your best options for engendering confidence in the content and quality of your books. An alliance with a Christian publishers association is a good place to start.

Joining a publishers association is a wise decision for any publisher. Here are four fundamental benefits of joining a publishers association.

1. You gain respect in the book industry.

In the Christian marketplace, name recognition for creditability purposes is probably the most important reason for a new, small, or self-publisher to join a Christian publishers association. Christian retailers gain confidence in a new publisher's products when they know that publisher is a member of a Christian organization in the industry. Professional organizations hold their members to a high standard of conduct. Membership in a professional association says,

"I am serious about my vocation." Don't you prefer to go to a doctor who is a member of the American Medical Association? Knowing that your doctor belongs to a professional organization makes you feel more secure that she is serious about learning and knowing the latest medical techniques. As a publisher, your membership in a publishers association brings you the same professional respect in the book industry. Book reviews are an essential ingredient in promoting a new title. Membership in a publishers association lends your publishing company credibility with book review sources. One example of this is The Midwest Book Review. This review source specializes in reviewing titles from small publishers, self-publishers, academic publishers, and specialty presses. However, they give priority consideration to those titles from publishers that belong to a publishers association.

2. You receive cutting-edge information.

Publishers associations provide their members with some form of regular communication (usually a newsletter) containing the latest developments and resources in the publishing industry. Many hold seminars and conferences to further their members' education and expertise in publishing issues. The information you glean from belonging to a publishers association can improve your business and bring you more success in your endeavors. Knowing what is currently working for other publishers helps you learn what to do to sell more copies of your books.

3. You save money.

Joining a professional publishers association costs money. However, if you take advantage of the many membership benefits these associations offer (which can include discounts on shipping costs, co-op marketing opportunities, health insurance programs for self-employed individuals, and liability insurance), you will save money in the long run. Some small publishers claim that the money they have saved on a freight discount benefit alone more than pays for their annual membership fees in one publishers association.

4. Doors of opportunity open for you.

Professional publishers associations provide many opportunities for you to network with other professionals in the book industry. Aside from the aforementioned seminars or conferences to attend, some associations also provide an online discussion group for member publishers. These opportunities allow you not only to find out what is working for other publishers but they lend you a venue to share your expertise.

Networking in this manner can also lead to other prospects such as a co-publishing agreement. Displaying your titles at a trade convention can lead to great deals. While generally a costly endeavor, some publishers associations provide opportunities for you to affordably display your titles. Some small publishers have sold international rights for their books through displaying titles at the Frankfurt Book Fair through a publishers association.

There are currently four professional publishers associations for those publishing materials for the Christian marketplace.

- **Catholic Book Publishers Association (CBPA)**

    CBPA is for publishers publishing materials for the Catholic marketplace. While not exclusively for the small publisher, they do have a sliding membership fee based on the size of the publishing house. CBPA produces a newsletter, provides co-op marketing opportunities, sponsors seminars, and gives publisher service awards.

    www.cbpa.org

- **Christian Small Publishers Association (CSPA)**
    CSPA is a newer organization for small and self-publishers publishing materials for the Christian marketplace. CSPA produces an e-newsletter, offers co-op advertising, exhibits members' books at Christian trade conventions, and offers distribution and credit card payment processing programs for their members.
    www.christianpublishers.net

- **Evangelical Christian Publishers Association (ECPA)**
    ECPA is a publishers association for established Christian publishers. It has the highest membership fee of the Christian publishers associations. ECPA considers a small publisher one with annual revenues under one million dollars. To become a member of ECPA, an existing ECPA publisher member must recommend you for membership.
    www.ecpa.org

- **Protestant Church-Owned Publishers Association (PCPA)**
    PCPA is an association of not-for-profit official Protestant church-owned publishing houses, directly connected to their respective denominations. PCPA supports publishers as they serve congregations within their denominations.
    www.pcpanews.org

Even if you publish only Christian materials, you don't have to limit yourself to just Christian publishers associations. Most bookstores and public libraries today offer many religious titles for their patrons. Additional membership in a general market publishers association can provide you information and cost-saving marketing opportunities to reach the general book market also.

Here is a list of general market publishers associations for small and self-publishers.

- **Publishers Marketing Association (PMA)**
    PMA publishes a newsletter, sponsors seminars, provides co-op promotional mailings, exhibits members' books at trade conventions, and sponsors the annual Benjamin Franklin Awards for the best books of the year published by independent publishers.
    www.pma-online.org

- **Small Publishers Association of North America (SPAN)**
    SPAN publishes a newsletter, offers co-op advertising and display opportunities, sponsors an annual conference, and hosts an online discussion group for small and self-publishers.
    www.spannet.org

- **Small Publishers, Artists, and Writers Network (SPAWN)**
    SPAWN provides opportunities for everyone involved in publishing. SPAWN encourages the exchange of ideas, information, and other mutual benefits.
    www.spawn.org

Join as many associations as you feel will gain you optimal information and the opportunities you need to be as successful as you desire in your publishing endeavors. Once you join a publishers association, make sure to include your membership in that association on your letterhead, your website, your press releases, and all your advertising materials to take full advantage of the name recognition and respect your membership brings you.

Subscribe to Industry Publications

A number of publications help publishers and authors stay abreast of current news and trends in the Christian marketplace. Some of these publications are more costly than others. However, there are a number of free e-newsletters that provide condensed news of the industry for those publishers and authors on a tight budget.

1. Subscription Publications

You do not need to subscribe to all of these publications to stay abreast of industry conditions. Since the Christian marketplace is a relatively small subset of publishing, information is often repeated between the publications listed here. A subscription to one of these publications complemented with the free e-newsletters listed below is generally sufficient to stay abreast of industry news.

- *Publishers Weekly*

    The most costly of these publications, *Publishers Weekly*, is the preeminent magazine for publishers and booksellers. *Publishers Weekly* covers the general book publishing market but includes a great deal of information on the religious marketplace. It is a weekly magazine.
    www.publishersweekly.com

- *Christian Retailing*

    Produced by Strang Publications, this magazine has been published for over 50 years. The magazine is free to Christian retail stores, but industry suppliers must pay for the periodical. *Christian Retailing* is produced bi-weekly.
    www.christianretailing.com

- *Aspiring Retail*

    Aspiring Retail is the official publication of CBA (Christian Booksellers Association). This monthly publication is free to all members of CBA. Non-members must pay a subscription fee.

    www.aspiringretail.com

- *BookWire Christian Publishing News & Reviews*

    This new publication, a joint venture of ECPA (Evangelical Christian Publishers Association) and R.R. Bowker, LLC, is set to launch in September 2006. Published quarterly, this magazine will feature news and information affecting the publishing and selling of Christian books, as well as articles on issues, opportunities, and new technologies shaping the Christian publishing industry.

    www.bowker.com
    www.bookwire.com

2. Free e-Newsletters

The beauty of e-newsletters is that they are the most cost-effective means of staying abreast of industry news. Most of the subscription publications listed above also offers a weekly e-newsletter free of charge. Simply sign up for the newsletter on each publication's website and you will receive the newsletter each week in your email inbox.

- *Religion BookLine*

    This is *Publishers Weekly*'s e-newsletter providing updates on religion publishing and book buying.

    www.publishersweekly.com

- **Christian Retailing e-Newsletter**
    Produced by *Christian Retailing*, this weekly e-newsletter features industry news for the Christian marketplace.
    www.christianretailing.com

- **CBA e-News**
    CBA (Christian Booksellers Association) produces this weekly e-newsletter featuring headline news for the Christian publishing and bookselling industry.
    www.cbaonline.org

Join Online Discussion Groups

Another good way to get connected, network, and learn from other publishers is to join online discussion groups for publishers. Joining discussion groups is free and it is a good avenue for acquiring information, ideas, and trends from other publishers. A sampling of online discussion groups for publishers is offered here.

- **Christian Small Publishers**
    Sponsored by CSPA (Christian Small Publishers Association), Christian Small Publishers is for small publishers who publish materials for the Christian marketplace. The group is designed to provide a forum for networking and discussing issues related to publishing and marketing in the Christian marketplace.
    http://groups.yahoo.com/group/christianpublishers

- **Christian Self-Publishing**
    This discussion group is for authors and small presses who are involved in self-publishing and marketing material to the

homeschooling or Christian private school markets. This list is run by Harvey and Laurie Bluedorn of Trivium Pursuit.
http://groups.yahoo.com/group/ChristianSelf-Publishing

- **Self-Publishing**
    Sponsored by SPAN (Small Publishers Association of North America), this discussion forum is a community of authors and small presses interested or involved in self-publishing and book marketing for the general marketplace.
    http://finance.groups.yahoo.com/group/self-publishing

- **Publish-L**
    This email discussion group is for issues related to publishing. It is a forum for the exchange of ideas and information about publishing and marketing books to the general marketplace. Anyone interested in publishing or engaged in the industry is welcome.
    www.publish-l.com

- **Ind-e-Pubs**
    A group for independent publishers currently involved or interested in being involved in e-publishing. Discussion mostly covers general market e-publishing issues.
    www.ind-e-pubs.com

- **POD Publishers**
    POD Publishers is a business discussion group for publishers of print-on-demand books. This group is primarily comprised of general market POD publishers.
    http://finance.groups.yahoo.com/group/pod_publishers

Connections for Christian Authors

For Christian authors, staying abreast of the industry is very important for you to effectively promote your books. Keeping informed about industry trends also helps you be aware of the types of materials the marketplace needs so you can be successful in your next writing project. Publishers should encourage their authors to stay connected with other Christian authors in the Christian marketplace. Here are a few ways authors can get connected.

1. Join a Christian Writers Association
A number of Christian writers associations exist to support, encourage, educate, and inform writers writing for the Christian marketplace.

- **American Christian Fiction Writers Association (ACFW)**
    Membership in ACFW provides Christian writers access to a monthly e-zine, critique groups, mentor groups, access to the ACFW online forum, and promotional opportunities for published authors.
    www.americanchristianfictionwriters.com

- **American Christian Writers Association (ACW)**
    ACW offers regional writers conferences around the country, regional charters providing local writers groups, and two publications: *Christian Communicator* and *Advanced Christian Writer*. Membership in ACW is not required to access any of these great services. Subscriptions are available for the association's two print publications.
    www.acwriters.com

- **Christian Writers Fellowship International (CWFI)**

    CWFI is a multi-service ministry to Christians in publishing. Member benefits include a bi-monthly newsletter, *Cross & Quill*; local Christian writers groups around the country; a critique service; and an online discussion group.

    www.cwfi-online.org

- **Fellowship of Christian Writers (FCW)**

    Located in Tulsa, Oklahoma, FCW began as a local Christian writers ministry, but is now available to writers at large. Membership provides a monthly newsletter; access to local writers groups featuring speakers, workshops, and critique groups; and entry into their writing contest. FCW also hosts an online discussion group that is open to any Christian writer. Membership in FCW is not required to participate in the discussion group.

    www.fellowshipofchristianwriters.org

- **Writers Information Network (WIN)**

    WIN is a professional association for Christian writers. The organization provides its members with a bi-monthly magazine, WIN-Informer, and seeks to furnish its members with up-to-date market information on religious book and magazine publishers. WIN also provides a referral system for connecting WIN members who are seeking speaking engagements with organizations in need of speakers for events.

    www.christianwritersinfo.net

2. Attend Christian Writers Conferences

Writers conferences provide you excellent opportunities to meet and connect with other Christian authors as well as to stay abreast of the industry trends. More Christian writers conferences take place across the United States each year than can be mentioned here. The most comprehensive listing of Christian conferences around the country can be found online at www.stuartmarket.com/conferences.html.

3. Join Online Author Discussion Groups

Another good way to get connected, network, and learn from others is to join online discussion groups for Christian authors. Joining discussion groups is free and it is a good avenue for acquiring encouragement and information. A sampling of online discussion groups for Christian authors is offered here.

- **ChristianWriters.com (CW)**

    The CW community includes a number of forums or discussion boards and a chat room for Christian authors. This group requires membership, but membership is free and easy to obtain online.

    www.christianwriters.com

- **Christian Writers Group (CWG)**

    CWG offers an online discussion group as well as a message board for Christian writers.

    www.christianwritersgroup.org

- **FaithWriters.com**

    FaithWriters also requires membership, but membership is free and easy to obtain online. This community provides message boards and discussion forums as well as other opportunities for writers to network and grow.

    www.faithwriters.com

- **Christian Electronic Authors**

    Owned by Christian e-Author, this group discusses electronic publishing and inspirational writing for electronic books. They investigate inspirational writing, promotional opportunities for electronic books, e-publishers, and the world of electronic publishing.

    http://groups.yahoo.com/group/Christian-e-author

Summary

C.S. Lewis once said, "The next best thing to being wise oneself is to live in a circle of those who are." Being a member of an association or discussion group places you in a circle of wise people. Associating with and learning from other people in your field helps you become wiser in your own business.

Secure Distribution 2

Of making many books there is no end.
—*Ecclesiastes 12:12*

DISTRIBUTION IS KEY TO REACHING the Christian retail marketplace. Even with name recognition, favorable Christian reviews, an ambitious marketing campaign, and a book award, without adequate distribution to the Christian retail market, a book will remain in your warehouse. A book must be easily accessible to retailers through established distribution channels to ensure retail orders. When a book is not readily available through the established distribution channels, retailers are less likely to pursue purchasing the title. The momentum you build through a fantastic marketing plan can easily be lost when your book is not readily available in retail channels.

Most Christian retailers prefer to order their products from a handful of sources. The fewer accounts they have to open and maintain, the easier their bookkeeping. A number of smaller orders to individual publishers generally results in more overhead and shipping costs for a store, which decreases the store's profit margin.

It is best to have your distribution channel established prior to the publication of your book. When submitting your title for trade announcements and book reviews, it is important to let the book industry know that your book will be available for retail orders through readily accepted channels in the marketplace. Having distribution also helps secure reviewers' confidence in your product and increases the likelihood that your book will be evaluated for review.

Two main choices exist for making your book readily available to the Christian retail marketplace: wholesale book companies and distributors.

Wholesale book companies purchase books from publishing companies and fulfill book orders from retail stores. Wholesale companies generally purchase books outright from a publisher, but will debit the publisher's account when retailers return unsold books. These companies generally purchase books from a publisher at a 55% to 60% discount off the retail price with some requiring the publisher to pay the shipping for books sold to the wholesale company. The wholesale company then sells the books to retail stores and libraries at a 40% to 45% discount.

Wholesale book companies provide no sales representation for the books they offer to retail outlets. All sales and marketing representation is the responsibility of the publishing company. Publishers must direct retail buyers to the wholesale company for ease of purchase. Wholesale companies offer publishers opportunities to advertise in their catalogs and other promotional materials that they send to bookstores and libraries on a regular basis. Wholesale companies generally want to know the specifics of a publisher's marketing plans, advertising budget, and sales representation for titles prior to agreeing to purchase and stock a new publisher's titles.

Distributors purchase books from publishing companies and sell these books to wholesalers, retail stores, and libraries. They provide sales representation (mostly to the larger and major chain bookstores) to promote the titles they sell. Most distributors purchase books from a publisher at a 65% to 70% discount off the retail price and some have the publisher pay for shipping the books to the distributor. The distributor then sells the books to the marketplace at a 40% to 45% discount.

Distributors usually work on a consignment basis, only paying publishers for books they have sold. Most require publishers to pay storage costs for the books they hold in their warehouse. Distributors will make the books they sell available for purchase through the major wholesale book companies to ensure more retail orders. Generally, distributors operate under "exclusive" contracts, meaning that they handle all sales to the retail marketplace (publisher cannot sell directly to retail outlets). Although distributors provide some sales representation they still expect publishers to continue to finance and run marketing campaigns for the books.

Christian Wholesale Book Companies

Currently there are three major wholesale book companies that focus directly on the Christian retail market. Almost all Christian bookstores have an account with one or more of these wholesalers and purchase books from them on a regular basis.

It is difficult for a new, emerging publisher in the Christian marketplace to secure an account with one of the three major Christian wholesale book companies. Spring Arbor requires that a publisher have a minimum of ten titles in print. The other two companies are more likely to accept a new publisher if that publishing company is advertising in one of the Christian retail marketing groups' promotional catalogs (see Chapter 6 for more information on Christian retail marketing groups).

- **Anchor Distributors**

    Anchor is the smallest of the three Christian wholesale book companies.

    1030 Hunt Valley Circle
    New Kensington, PA 15068
    800-444-4484
    purchasing@anchordistributors.com
    www.anchordistributors.com

- **Appalachian Distributors, Inc.**

    Appalachian is owned by STL (Send the Light, Ltd.).

    522 Princeton Road
    P.O. Box 1573
    Johnson City, TN 37601
    Kim Williams, Director of Purchasing
    800-289-2772
    kwilliams@appalink.com
    www.appalink.com

- **Spring Arbor Distributors, Inc.**

    Spring Arbor is the largest of the three wholesale companies. It is Ingram Book Group's Christian division. A publisher must have a minimum of 10 titles in print for Spring Arbor to consider purchasing and stocking titles. Publishers with less than 10 titles are encouraged to contract with a distributor to ensure that their title is available through Spring Arbor. When your title is accepted by Spring Arbor, it is also

available for retailers and librarians to order through Ingram's general market book channel.
bookbuyer@ingrambook.com
http://www.ingrambook.com/new/publishers.asp

Due to the difficulty of accessing wholesale distribution services for new publishers with few titles, Christian Small Publishers Association (CSPA) offers their member publishers the benefit of a distribution program for stocking titles with Spring Arbor.

General Market Wholesale Book Companies

For small and self-publishers that wish to make their titles available for order by the general market bookstores and librarians, having titles stocked with a general market wholesale book company is essential. There are a number of wholesale book companies for the general market. The two largest are mentioned here.

- **Baker & Taylor, Inc.**

    Baker & Taylor sells books to the general retail market and the general library market. Baker & Taylor will accept small publishers' titles; however, there is a fee to join Baker & Taylor as a publisher supplier.

    For most small publishers, Baker & Taylor lists their titles as available for purchase by retailer and librarians, but does not purchase the title from the publisher until a retail store or library places an order for the title. This can add up to larger shipping costs for small publishers when book orders from Baker & Taylor trickle in one or two books at a time.

    Baker & Taylor requires that new publishers submit an application and they will then contact the publisher with

additional information. The application to become a publisher supplier with Baker & Taylor can be found online.
www.btol.com/supplier_info.cfm

- **Ingram Book Group**
    Ingram Book Group sells books to the general retail market and the general library market. A publisher must have a minimum of 10 titles in print for Ingram to consider purchasing and stocking titles.
    bookbuyer@ingrambook.com
    http://www.ingrambook.com/new/publishers.asp

Christian Marketplace Distributors

Many large Christian publishing houses have distribution departments that provide sales representation and order fulfillment for Christian retail stores and churches. Some large Christian publishing houses distribute for other Christian publishers who choose not to conduct their own sales and order fulfillment. There are a few distributors in the Christian marketplace who provide sales representation and order fulfillment for large and medium size Christian publishing houses. These distributors include Noble Marketing Group (www.noblemktg.com), CNI Distribution (www.cnidist.com), and GL Services' Inspirational Publishers Group (IPG) (www.glservices.com).

Currently, there are three main distributors for the Christian marketplace that specialize in and work with small and self-publishers. Two of these distributors require an exclusive contract for the retail and library marketplace.

Each sells the titles they carry to the major wholesale book companies and provides some type of sales presentation to Christian chain bookstores as well as at some Christian tradeshows.

- **AtlasBooks Distribution Service**
    AtlasBooks, a division of BookMasters, Inc., requires an exclusive contract.
    2541 Ashland Rd.
    P.O. Box 2139
    Mansfield, OH 44905
    800-537-6727
    info@atlasbooks.com
    www.atlasbooks.com

- **FaithWorks**
    This company, owned by STL (as is Appalachian) requires an exclusive contract for the retail and library marketplace.

    9247 Hunterboro Dr.
    Brentwood, TN 37027
    615-221-6442
    Contact: Larry Carpenter
    lcarpenter@faithworksonline.com
    www.faithworksonline.com

- **WinePress Promotions**
    WinePress Promotions, a division of WinePress Publishing, offers order fulfillment and distribution.

    WinePress Promotions
    Product Review Board
    1730 Railroad St.
    Enumclaw, WA 98022
    800-326-4674
    www.wppromotions.com

Summary

One of the biggest mistakes new small or self-publishers can make is to neglect the distribution aspect of their marketing plan. Securing distribution sends a signal to the book trade industry that you are serious about marketing your books. Having national distribution through a distributor or wholesale book company selling books to the Christian marketplace is vital for securing book reviews and book orders from the Christian marketplace.

Announce Your Books 3

The words of the wise are like goads, their collected sayings like firmly embedded nails—given by one Shepherd.
—*Ecclesiastes 12:11*

ANNOUNCING A NEW BOOK is a way to get the public interested in your upcoming title even before it hits the street. Publishers have a small window of opportunity to announce and promote new titles to the book industry (retailers, librarians, and book reviewers). The book industry is always looking for the next new book. Announcements of new titles catch the industry's attention and generate interest much more successfully than those titles that have been around for awhile.

Trade announcements let you unveil your title to the marketplace prior to publication alerting retailers, librarians, and book reviewers of your upcoming title. Generally, trade announcements are made three to six months prior to the release of your title. Take advantage of the opportunities in the Christian marketplace for announcing an upcoming title since these announcements are both free and a prudent marketing strategy.

Christian Books Database

When you assign an ISBN to a book, R.R. Bowker, the ISBN agency, requests that you register your ISBN and the title of the book so that they can include the book in their Books in Print database. Bowker's Books in Print database strives to be a comprehensive listing of all books containing ISBNs in the marketplace. The Christian marketplace has its own versions of Bowker's Books in Print for Christian titles.

- **Christian Books & More Database**

    This database is to the Christian retail market what Bowker's Books in Print is to the general booksellers market. Christian Books & More strives to provide a complete list of all Christian products for sale to the Christian retail market. It is free to list products in Christian Books & More Database.

    Christian Books & More Database is used by over 1,200 Christian stores for ordering and tracking product. It is also used to power some of the online Christian bookstore search engines such as Parable.com®.

    If you are marketing a book to the Christian retail marketplace, it is essential to get it listed in Christian Books & More Database. Instructions for submitting titles are available on their website.
    database@bsmgr.com
    www.bookstoremanager.com/vendor/cbm.aspx

- **International Christian Book Database**

    This database is sponsored by Global Publishers Alliance (GPA), a division of Evangelical Christian Publishers Association (ECPA) in cooperation with the Network for

Strategic Missions. For a book to be eligible for listing in this database, the following four criteria must be met:

1. Must be a Christian book.
2. Must be published in a language other than English.
3. Must be available through an overseas distributor or online on the World Wide Web.
4. The publisher must be a member of ECPA (Evangelical Christian Publishers Association) or CSPA (Christian Small Publishers Association).

The database can be accessed through the Network for Strategic Missions, a website that provides resources to missionaries around the world. Visit www.strategicnetwork.org and click on "Books" to view the database.

Along with their database for international Christian books, GPA would also like to see Christian publishers standardize the names and codes for the languages in which their books are printed. To this end, GPA is encouraging publishers to use the Ethnologue Languages of the World published by SIL International, which provides over 6,000 language names and attaches a three-letter code to each language name for uniform identification of all known human languages. Visit www.ethnologue.com/codes to find the complete list of languages and their corresponding codes.

Christian Retail Magazines

Currently, there are two magazines designed for Christian retailers on the market and both include some coverage of upcoming titles in addition to their product reviews. Name recognition is just as important for the editors of these Christian retail magazines as it is for Christian retailers. Therefore, when submitting a press release about your upcoming title, if your book is not by a known Christian personality, make sure that you include your membership in a Christian publishers association, your distribution for the Christian retail market, and other pertinent data providing assurance of a quality Christian product.

- ***Aspiring Retail***

    This magazine is produced by CBA (Christian Booksellers Association) for Christian retailers. A subscription to *Aspiring Retail* is included with a retailer's CBA membership.
    www.aspiringretail.com

    Press releases for editorial review and inclusion in *Aspiring Retail* should be submitted to:
    - Lynn Waalkes at lwaalkes@cbaonline.org for adult books
    - Lisa Tamayo at ltamayo@cbaonline.org for children's books

- ***Christian Retailing***

    Produced by Strang Communications, this publication is geared toward Christian retailers, as all information in the magazine revolves around the Christian retail marketplace. The magazine is free to any bookstore actively selling Christian products in the United States.
    www.christianretailing.com

    Press releases for editorial review and inclusion in *Christian Retailing* should be submitted to:

- Chris Johnson at chris.johnson@strang.com for adult books
- Karen Schmidt at krnschmidt@earthlink.net for children's books
- Terry Walsh at terrywalsh@walsh-group.com for Catholic/liturgical books

Other Trade Announcements

There are some general market publications that offer free upcoming title announcements. Take advantage of these free listings for your Christian titles also. While these publications are not strictly for the Christian marketplace, many Christian retailers keep abreast of the larger book industry as well as the Christian industry and thus subscribe to these publications. Since many general market bookstores carry religious titles and exposure is an essential element in a book's success, submitting your title to these listings is sensible marketing.

- *Publisher's Weekly (PW)*

    PW is the number one trade journal of the publishing industry. Used widely by publishers, book reviewers, retailers, and librarians, it is produced on a weekly basis and covers all the current news for the publishing industry. *Publisher's Weekly* features spring and fall book announcements for adult books, children's books, and religious books.
    www.publishersweekly.com

    PW's Religious Book Announcements include religion/spirituality/inspirational and children's religious books. Lynn Garrett is the religion editor for *PW*. She edits the twice yearly Religion Announcements. Contact her to request to be placed on the mailing list to receive submission notices for the spring and fall Religion Announcements.

- Contact Lynn Garrett at 847-328-4043 or lgarrett@reedbusiness.com

- *ForeWord Magazine*

    ForeWord Magazine is a trade review journal devoted exclusively to covering books from small and independent publishing houses. *ForeWord Magazine* showcases upcoming titles in its Seasonal Announcements twice yearly. The March/April edition features Spring Announcements and the July/August edition features Fall Announcements. Submission of a title is required three months in advance. Title submissions are made online at *ForeWord Magazine*'s website.
    www.forewordmagazine.com.

- *Library Journal*

    This journal is an adult book review publication for public and academic librarians. They also feature upcoming title announcements for spring and fall in two issues throughout the year. Their editorial calendar on their website provides information on which issues the announcements appear in and submission deadlines.
    www.libraryjournal.com

    For more information on how to submit a title for announcement, contact:
    - Tania Barnes at 646-746-6818 or email her at tbarnes@reedbusiness.com

- *Booklist*

    This monthly publication of the American Library Association provides reviews of books for librarians across the country. They also feature seasonal book announcements for new titles. Send *Booklist* four copies (this can be in the form of a brochure, catalog, or media release) of the title announcement for your upcoming book.
    www.ala.org/booklist

    Title announcements should be addressed to:
    - Brad Hooper at bhooper@ala.org for adult books
    - Stephanie Zvirin at szvirin@ala.org for young adult and children's books

- *Small Press Record of Books in Print*

    Produced annually by Dustbooks, this record is a listing of books in print by small and self-publishers. Title submission can be made online on their website.
    www.dustbooks.com

Other Announcements

Announcing a book to generate interest and buzz about your upcoming title is an important part of a marketing plan.

When announcing your book, you shouldn't overlook the various publishers or writers associations of which you are a member. Send your new book announcements to these organizations as most publishers and writers associations include new book announcements in the newsletter or journal they produce for their members.

Also, don't forget to alert the members of the discussion groups you belong to about your new title. Discussion groups generally allow you to post new book announcements for the group.

If you have a mailing list of customers who have previously purchased books from your publishing company, use this list to generate a pre-publication announcement for your new titles. Whether you mail a postcard, letter, or brochure, or send an email announcement, make sure to include ordering information in your notice. New book announcements sent via email or snail mail to your established customers will result in more orders for your new titles.

Garner Book Reviews   4

Let another praise you, and not your own mouth;
someone else, and not your own lips.

—*Proverbs 27:2*

BOOK REVIEWS ARE AN ESSENTIAL ELEMENT of any book launch and marketing campaign. Reviews generate the interest of book buyers and provide publishers with a great low-cost marketing tool. For the cost of a book and postage, a review can supply praise and exposure for your books.

Favorable reviews by reputable review sources provide your book recognition in the Christian marketplace. Reviews also bring broader exposure for your titles. Every publication providing reviews of books has a membership base reading it for those reviews. A review in a publication geared toward the Christian marketplace exposes all of its readers to your title. Even an unfavorable review will still provide exposure. In fact, sometimes unfavorable reviews actually drive more people to a book, especially if the opinion of the reviewer sparks controversy about the book's topic.

A complimentary review by a reputable review source is gold to a publisher. Every review a book secures can be used repeatedly in your marketing campaign. Favorable reviews (or elements of a review) should be posted on your website, printed on all your marketing materials, used in advertisements, and added to your book's cover on subsequent print runs.

Reviews of books tend to be broken down into two categories: trade reviews and reviews for consumers. Trade reviews are reviews geared toward the retail marketplace. These reviews alert retailers and librarians of upcoming books and provide a short synopsis of the book with an opinion (by the reviewer) as to how the book will be received by consumers. Reviews for consumers are similar to industry trade reviews except that they are geared to book buyers and readers. Consumer reviews also provide a short synopsis of the book and an opinion (by the reviewer) on whether the book is worth investing the time to read it.

Materials to Include When Submitting a Galley or Book for Review

Presentation is important in every aspect of marketing books, including submissions for review. The following items are the essential elements for a book review request package.

- **A Cover Letter**

    The information you provide in the cover letter should include the title of the book, the author, the book's category, the publisher, the ISBN, book binding, retail price, number of illustrations and pages, the publication date, any distributors, and your overall marketing plan for the book. Having both distribution and a strong marketing plan boosts your chances of being reviewed. Review publications prefer to review books that they feel will sell well, and the stronger the marketing plan, the greater the chances a book will sell (and, therefore, that you'll get a review).

- **A Fact Sheet or a Press Release**

    A fact sheet or press release should summarize how your book is distinctive and different from other books. It should also contain the exact title of the book, the author's name, publication date, ISBN, retail price, contact information for the publisher of the book, and ordering information. Including a section on the author's credentials for writing the book and including the names of other books by the author adds credence to your book. Outlines and samples of press releases can be found online at PRWeb Press Release Newswire.

    www.prweb.com/pressreleasetips.php

- **The Actual Book or Galley**

    Most review publications specify whether they want one or two copies of either the galley or the actual book to review. Those requesting galleys require that they be sent three to four months in advance of publication (the date your book becomes available for sale), while those desiring the actual book to review expect to get the book within the first few months of the publication date. A galley is typically a bound typeset proof of a book in page format that includes a generic cover containing all the important facts about the book.

Christian Trade Reviews

When submitting a galley for review by a Christian trade review source, send a query to the reviewer describing your book prior to sending the actual galley. Make sure you include all information necessary to secure the reviewer's confidence that you have a reputable Christian product. Information in a query should include any endorsements by known Christian personalities, any Christian publishers association memberships, a thumbnail sketch of your marketing plans, and who will be distributing the book to the Christian marketplace. The reviewer will then let you know if they are interested in reviewing your book, saving you time as well as wasted books (or galleys) and postage.

- *Aspiring Retail*

    This publication reviews galleys at least three months prior to publication date.

    Contact:
    - Lynn Waalkes at lwaalkes@cbaonline.org for adult book reviews
    - Lisa Tamayo at ltamayo@cbaonline.org for children's book reviews

    CBA International
    Aspiring Retail
    P.O. Box 62000
    Colorado Springs, CO 80962-2000
    719-265-9895
    www.aspiringretail.com

- *Christian Retailing*

    This magazine reviews galleys at least three months prior to publication date.

Contact:
- Chris Johnson at chris.johnson@strang.com for general book reviews
- Karen Schmidt at krnschmidt@earthlink.net for children's book reviews
- Terry Walsh at terrywalsh@walsh-group.com for Catholic/liturgical reviews

Strang Communications
Christian Retailing
600 Rinehart Rd.
Lake Mary, FL 32746
407-333-0600
www.christianretailing.com

- ***BookWire Christian Publishing News & Reviews***

This new quarterly publication, a joint venture of ECPA (Evangelical Christian Publishers Association) and R.R. Bowker, LLC, is set to launch in September 2006. It will be mailed free of charge to over 12,000 book professionals including general market librarians and book buyers. Publishers can submit manuscripts for review by a team of highly knowledgeable Christian professionals within the industry. Book reviews are provided for a fee (similar to R.R. Bowker's existing *Bookwire Review* service).

Contact:
- Josephine Murphy at josephine.murphy@bowker.com for information on submitting manuscripts for review

R.R. Bowker
630 Central Ave.
New Providence, NJ 07974
1-800-521-8110
www.bookwire.com / www.bowker.com

General Trade Reviews

The following trade review sources include reviews of religious titles in their publications. While these trade reviews are geared toward the general book market, they are reputable review sources and recognized as such by Christian retailers. It is always wise to query the reviewer for these publications prior to mailing your books for review.

Most of these publications have their submission criteria listed on their webpage. Some do not want publishers to contact them prior to submitting a book for review. These publications receive so many books to review that they prefer less communication. Some provide a contact to use after your submission is sent and others request that you do not contact them after submission; they will contact you if your book is chosen for review. Since book reviews are a low-cost marketing effort, submitting titles for review is always a prudent marketing tactic (even to the larger review publications) as you never know when your book may be chosen for a review.

Some review publications request that you submit more than one copy of your title in galley or book form. The publications that request galleys usually also request that you submit copies of the actual book when it becomes available. This is really only necessary for those publications that are providing a review of your title.

- **Black Issues Book Review**

  This magazine is the premiere African-American book publishing authority. It provides reviews of fiction and non-fiction books by Black authors.

  Black Issues Book Review
  Empire State Building
  350 Fifth Ave., Suite 1522
  New York, NY 10118
  212-947-8515
  www.bibookreview.com

- **Booklist**

  This publication of the American Library Association provides reviews of books for librarians across the country. Submit galleys only to:

  - Brad Hooper, Adult Books Editor, at bhooper@ala.org for adult books
  - Stephanie Zvirin, Books for Youth Editor, at szvirin@ala.org for young adult and children's books

  Booklist
  American Library Association
  50 E. Huron
  Chicago, IL 60611
  www.ala.org/booklist

- **BookPage**

  BookPage: America's Book Review provides reviews of books for booksellers and librarians. This publication reviews all types of books except for poetry, print-on-demand and self-published titles. Submit galleys to:

- Lynn Green, Editor at www@bookpage.com for adult books
- Children's Editor at www@bookpage.com for children's titles

BookPage
2143 Belcourt Ave.
Nashville, TN 37212
www.bookpage.com

- ***ForeWord Magazine***

This bi-monthly pre-publication review journal has a circulation of around 20,000 booksellers, librarians, and industry professionals. The magazine provides reviews of books published by small and independent publishing houses. *ForeWord Magazine* matches their print review with the month of the publication date of the title, so they only accept galleys three to four months in advance of publication date. Submit galleys to:

Alex Moore
Managing Editor
ForeWord Magazine
129 1/2 East Front Street
Traverse City, MI 49684
Alex@forewordmagazine.com
www.forewordmagazine.com/reviews/guidelines.aspx

- ***The Horn Book Magazine* and *Horn Book Guide***

    These distinguished journals only review young adult and children's literature. *The Horn Book Magazine* is published bi-monthly. *The Horn Book Guide* is published semi-annually. These publications require two copies of new titles to be sent for review to:

    The Horn Book, Inc.
    56 Roland Street, Suite 200
    Boston, MA 02129
    info@hbook.com
    www.hbook.com

- **Library Journal**

    This adult book review journal is for public and academic librarians. Submit galleys in advance of publication to:

    Book Review Editor
    Library Journal
    360 Park Avenue South
    New York, New York 10010
    www.libraryjournal.com

- **Midwest Book Review**

    The Midwest Book Review is an organization committed to promoting literacy, library usage, and small press publishing. They give consideration to small press publishers, self-published authors, academic presses, and specialty publishers. Several monthly publications are published by the Midwest Book Review for community and academic library systems. All reviews by the Midwest Book Review are posted on Internet forums as well as on Amazon.com®.

The Midwest Book Review only accepts books that are already in print and available to the public. Only published copies (no galleys or uncorrected proofs) are accepted for review. Submissions for review should be directed to:

James A. Cox
Editor-in-Chief
Midwest Book Review
278 Orchard Drive
Oregon, WI 53575
www.midwestbookreview.com

- *Publishers Weekly*

This is the number one trade journal of the publishing industry. Used widely by publishers, book reviewers, booksellers, and librarians, it is produced on a weekly basis and features reviews of new books. Submit two copies of your religious book galley three to four months prior to publication to:

Adult Religion Books
Jana Riess
3535 Waterworks Rd.
Winchester, KY 40391
859-744-5558
pwrelrevs@earthlink.net
www.publishersweekly.com

Children's Religion Books
Elizabeth Devereaux
360 Park Avenue South
New York, NY 10010

646-746-6772
www.publishersweekly.com

- *Small Press Review*

Published by Dustbooks, this monthly newsprint magazine features reviews of the latest small press books. Submit books for review to:

Len Fulton, Editor
Dustbooks
P.O. Box 100
Paradise, CA 95967
info@dustbooks.com
www.dustbooks.com

Reviews for Church Librarians

Large numbers of churches across the United States host a church library in their building for their members' reading enrichment. Church library associations exist to provide services and resources for these libraries. One of these services is the production of a newsletter or journal to encourage and educate church librarians. These publications all contain reviews of new books that might be of interest to the church libraries they reach.

Church library publications review books that are new (within a few months of publication date) rather than galleys. As with any book review request, it is wise to query editors with information about your book to make sure that your title fits with each publication's audience prior to submitting your book for review.

- ***ASDAL Action***

    This journal is published three times a year by the Association of Seventh Day Adventist Librarians.
    www.asdal.org

    - Contact scottrell@southern.edu for book review submission information

- ***Catholic Library World***

    The Catholic Library Association's official publication, this is published quarterly. Submit books for review to:

    CLA
    100 North Street, Suite 224
    Pittsfield, MA 01201-5109
    www.cathla.org

- ***Christian Library Journal***

    This online publication is geared toward both church and Christian school librarians. This publication is very open to reviewing materials from new and small publishers. They review only finished books.

    Nancy Hesch, Editor
    Christian Library Journal
    1225 Johnson St.
    Wenatchee, WA 98801
    509-662-7455
    nlhesch@christianlibraryj.org
    www.christianlibraryj.org

- *Church Libraries*

This publication is published quarterly by the Evangelical Church Library Association, a national organization for church and Christian school librarians. Materials approved for review must be published in the past year and be conservative, evangelical, and non-charismatic. *Church Libraries* does not review self-published books, ebooks, or print-on-demand books.

    Lin Johnson, Managing Editor
    Church Libraries
    9118 W Elmwood Dr #1G
    Niles, IL 60714-5820
    lin@eclalibraries.org.
    www.eclalibraries.org

- *Church & Synagogue LIBRARIES*

This is a bi-monthly publication of the Church and Synagogue Library Association, which serves congregational libraries of all faiths.

    Monica Tenney, Book Review Editor
    Church & Synagogue LIBRARIES
    P.O. Box 19357
    Portland, OR 97280
    motenney@aol.com
    http://cslainfo.org

- *The Lamplighter*

The Pacific Northwest Association of Church Libraries assists in the establishment and operation of church libraries

in the Pacific Northwest states. It produces *The Lamplighter* quarterly for its members.
www.pnacl.org

- Contact June Ruyle, Book Review Editor, at junepnacl@juno.com or Susan Reiver, *Lamplighter* Editor, at rprser@uswest.net.

- **Libraries Alive**

This quarterly publication of the National Church Library Association features book reviews as well as news of authors. This association was originally a Lutheran library association but now has expanded its services beyond just Lutheran Church libraries.

National Church Library Association
275 South Third Street, Suite 101A
Stillwater, MN 55082
651-430-0770
Info@churchlibraries.org
www.churchlibraries.org

Reviews for Christian Consumers

The two publications listed in this section review either galleys or newly published books for Christian readers. These publications are aimed at the general Christian marketplace and have large circulations. Many more Christian magazines exist for specific markets. (For more information on garnering reviews and coverage of your titles in Christian magazines, please refer to Chapter 8.)

As with trade reviews, whenever possible, query the book review editor first before submitting your book for review. Again, make sure you include all information necessary to secure the reviewer's confidence that you have a reputable Christian product readily available to readers in the marketplace.

- ***Books & Culture: A Christian Review / Christianity Today***

    Books & Culture is a bi-monthly review of books produced by Christianity Today International. The editor of *Books & Culture* is also the editor-at-large for *Christianity Today* magazine.

    > John Wilson, Editor
    > Christianity Today International
    > 465 Gundersen Dr.
    > Carol Stream, IL 60188
    > bceditor@booksandculture.com
    > www.booksandculture.com

- **WORLD *Magazine***

    This magazine provides weekly news from a Christian viewpoint. It is a Christian counterpart to general market news magazines like *Newsweek* and *Time*.

    > Contact:
    > - Marvin Olasky for youth and adult book reviews
    > - Susan Olasky for children's book reviews
    >
    > *World Magazine*
    > Box 20002
    > Asheville, NC 28802
    > www.worldmag.com

Online Christian Book Review Sites

More and more book review sites are cropping up online. These sites provide many additional opportunities to increase the exposure of your titles to Christian consumers, which generally amounts to more book sales. Most online Christian book review sites have steady clientele who frequent their site or at least receive the site's e-newsletter providing information on the latest Christian titles for their reading pleasure.

As with traditional print reviews, these websites only accept newly published books or pre-publication galleys to review. Most sites include their submission criteria or have a contact person listed for you to request the submission criteria.

- **General Christian Titles (both fiction and non-fiction)**
    - www.christianbookpreviews.com
    - www.faithfulreader.com
    - www.faithwebbin.net
    - www.dancingword.net/bookreviews.htm
    - www.mychurchlibrary.com
    - http://come.to/bookreviews

- **Christian Fiction Titles**
    - www.christianfictionreview.com
    - www.christianfictionsite.com
    - www.craighart.net
    - http://catswebdesigns.com/At_Home_with_Christian_Fiction
    - www.theromancereadersconnection.com – click on "Inspirational Corner"

- Christian Titles for Women
    - www.goodgirlbookclubonline.com

- African-American Christian Titles
    - http://marilynngriffith.typepad.com/word_praize/conference/index.html
    - http://www.blackbookreviews.com
    - www.qbr.com

- Christian Science Fiction / Fantasy
    - www.edenstarbooks.com
    - www.christianfantasy.net
    - www.pax-romana.net/refracted

After a Review

Jesus healed ten men with leprosy; only one remembered to return to thank him. Remember to be like the one. When you receive a book review, remember to send a thank you note to the reviewer. Not only is it polite and thoughtful, it will ingratiate you to the reviewer so that when your next title is placed in front of him, he will be more likely to take the time to review it.

Remember book reviews add credibility to your title, so post reviews on your website, use them in all your marketing and advertising materials, and include them in your book on the next print run. Reviews provide an independent opinion of your book for consumers to use when making a purchasing decision.

Pursue Book Awards 5

Do you see a man skilled in his work?
He will serve before kings; he will not serve before obscure men.
—*Proverbs 22:29*

BOOK AWARDS BRING EXPOSURE to books. Exposure generates sales. Sales mean more money in your pocket. Pursuing those book awards that allow publishers or authors to nominate their own titles can be beneficial.

While entering a book award contest is not a guaranteed win for your entry fee, it certainly more than pays off if your book is picked for an award. Some book award programs publish the runners-up as well as the award winners. If your book falls into either of these categories, you receive a marketing gem.

Book awards, like book reviews, can be harnessed to promote your title in endless ways. One benefit of a book award over a book review is that an award warrants press coverage. Newspapers, magazines, and newsletters like to highlight authors and books that have won awards. Another benefit of a book award is that consumers tend to want to read books that have won awards. An award tells a consumer that a book is worth the money to purchase and time spent to read it. An award signals booksellers to purchase the book for their stores as book awards almost always guarantee sales.

When a book award is bestowed, the award should be used repeatedly in your marketing campaign. In addition to alerting the press about a book award, any book award should be posted on your website, printed on all your marketing materials, used in advertisements, and added to your book's cover on subsequent print runs. Also, make sure that you let your distributors know about the award and send an announcement to those publishers associations and discussion groups where you are a member.

The literary community hosts a myriad of book awards. These awards differ as to who can nominate a book for an award. For some awards, publishers or authors can nominate their books and a committee or select group of people vote on the nominated titles. Other awards choose to have a nominating committee decide which titles should be considered for an award. Some awards have a select group of people (such as retailers, teachers, or students) nominate titles. There are a few book awards that are based on the number of copies a title has sold or lifetime achievements of an author. Generally, entry fees are charged for those awards that allow publishers and authors to nominate books.

Christian Book Awards

Christian book awards reflect the myriad of book awards available in the broader literary community. For some awards, publisher or author nomination is acceptable; for others, retailers nominate; and still others are based on sales figures.

- **American Academy of Religion Awards for Excellence**

    The American Academy of Religion (AAR) offers two Awards for Excellence: Best First Book in the History of Religions and Award for Excellence in the Study of Religion.

    The Best First Book in the History of Religions honors exceptional publications of first books published by nominees in the history of religion.

    Awards for Excellence in the Study of Religion recognize new works of books that affect decisively how religion is examined, understood, and interpreted. Awards in the Study of Religion are granted for three categories: Constructive-Reflective Study of Religion, Historical Study of Religion, and Analytical-Descriptive Study of Religion. Books can be nominated by any individual or institution.

    www.aarweb.org/awards/book/rules.asp.

- **American Christian Fiction Writers Book of the Year Awards**

    This award is given annually by American Christian Fiction Writers (ACFW) for Christian fiction works in eight categories. Awards are given only for books whose authors are members of American Christian Fiction Writers. Entry rules and forms are available for members on ACFW's website.

    www.americanchristianfictionwriters.com

- **Catholic Press Awards**

    Presented annually by the Catholic Press Association (CPA), these Catholic book awards are given for 18 categories including First Time Author, Children's, Spirituality, and a Spanish language category.

    www.catholicpress.org

- ***Christianity Today* Book Awards**

    Presented annually by *Christianity Today* magazine, these awards honor titles from 22 categories. Books are judged on their contributions to bringing understanding to people, events, and ideas that shape evangelical life and mission.

    Books are nominated by publishers. The staff of *Christianity Today* selects the top five books in each category and then panels of judges (one panel for each category) determine the winners.

    www.christianitytoday.com

- **Christy Awards**

    Christy Awards are presented annually to recognize and promote Christian fiction of an exceptional quality and impact. The awards feature a half-dozen fiction categories in which awards are presented: General/Contemporary, Historical, Romance, Suspense/Mystery, Visionary, and First Novel. The entry submission deadline for the Christy Awards is in December for books published during that calendar year.

    www.christyawards.com

- **ECPA Christian Book Awards**

    These awards, formerly named Gold Medallion Book Awards, are given annually by the Evangelical Christian Publishers Association (ECPA) for six categories. Designed to recognize the absolute highest quality in Christian books, the ECPA Christian Book Awards are the oldest and among the most prestigious in the religious publishing community. Nominations can only be made by ECPA member publishers in good standing. Publishers nominate their best books released in the previous calendar year.

    www.ecpa.org/awards.php

- **Gold, Platinum, Diamond, & Double Diamond Book Awards**

    Also awarded by ECPA, these book awards are based on sales figures for a title. They are designed to recognize outstanding sales achievement in the publication of quality Christian literature.

    Gold Book Awards are for books that have sold 500,000 copies, Platinum Book Awards are for titles which have achieved one million sales, Diamond Book Awards are for a book property selling 10 million copies, and Double Diamond Book Awards are for when a book property sells 20 million copies. A book does not have to be published by an ECPA member publishing house to qualify for these awards.

    www.ecpa.org/awards.php

- **Retailers Choice Awards**

    Retailers Choice Awards are sponsored by *Christian Retailing*. Products nominated for the annual Retailers Choice Awards must have been published and released in the previous year. Nominations are accepted from publishers and then Christian retailers vote on the list of nominated titles. They vote based on the impact the books have had on staff and customers, including a book's ability to speak to hearts and evoke emotion, open minds to new ways of thinking, and encourage and affirm Christ-like living.

    www.retailerschoiceawards.com

- **Theologos Awards**

    The Theologos Awards are given annually by the Association of Theological Booksellers (ATB) in five categories: Best General Interest Book, Best Academic Book, Best Children's Book, Book of the Year, and Publisher of the

Year. Only the bookseller members of the association are eligible to nominate and to vote.
http://associationoftheologicalbooksellers.org/theologos.html

General Book Awards with Religious Categories

A number of book awards exist in the general market literary community that are aimed at the independent, small, or self-publisher. Most of these book awards include at least one religious category. Each of the awards listed below accepts nominations from publishers and/or authors.

- **Annual *Writer's Digest* International Self-Published Book Awards**
    Sponsored by *Writer's Digest*, these book awards are the only awards exclusively for self-published books. Awards are offered in nine categories.
    www.writersdigest.com/contests

- **Ben Franklin Awards™**
    PMA (Publishers Marketing Association) sponsors the Ben Franklin Awards which are named in honor of America's most cherished publisher/printer. Books are judged on editorial and design merit by top practitioners in the field. Awards are presented for genre categories. Publishers must nominate titles.
    www.pma-online.org/benfrank.cfm

- **Best Book Awards**
    Sponsored by USABookNews.com, these awards feature over 80 categories including Religion and Religious Fiction.

Best Book Awards actively promote the winning titles through their website and through the media.
www.usabooknews.com

- **Indie Excellence National Book Awards**

    The Writers Marketing Association presents these awards for non-published manuscripts, POD books, and books by self-published or small press authors. Awards are presented in over 50 categories including Religion and Religious Fiction.
www.wmaconnect.com

- ***ForeWord Magazine*'s Book of the Year Award**

    ForeWord Magazine's Book of the Year Award was established to bring increased attention from librarians and booksellers to the literary achievements of independent publishers and their authors. The awards are presented in 60 categories including Religion and Religious Fiction. Print-on-demand titles and ebooks are accepted for nomination.
www.forewordmagazine.com/awards.asp

- **The Hurston/Wright Legacy Award™**

    This award, given by The Hurston/Wright Foundation and sponsored by Borders Books, is the first national award presented to published writers of African descent by the national community of Black writers. The award is offered for four categories and nominations must be submitted by the publisher with permission from the author.
www.hurstonwright.org/legacy_award.html

- **Independent Publisher Book Awards**

    The Independent Publisher Book Awards are sponsored by the Jenkins Group. These awards are for independent,

university, small press, and self-publishers who produce books intended for the North American market. Print-on-demand titles are acceptable. The award offers 60 award categories, including an Inspirational/Spiritual, a Religious Fiction, and a Religion category, as well as 10 regional awards for fiction and non-fiction books. Books must have a copyright or have been released in the previous year to be eligible for nomination.
www.independentpublisher.com

- **Writers Notes Annual Book Awards**
These awards are sponsored by *Writers Notes Magazine* to recognize extraordinary books by independent publishers. Awards in 11 categories are offered.
http://hopepubs.home.comcast.net/awards.html

Summary

Book awards abound in the literary community. Several websites contain fairly comprehensive lists of general market literary awards. These websites include:

www.literature-awards.com
www.bookreporter.com/features/awards.asp
www.bookwire.com/bookwire/otherbooks/Book-Awards.html

Section II

Selling Your Books

Reach Christian Retail Stores 6

And pray for us, too, that God may open a door for our message, so that we may proclaim the mystery of Christ.
—*Colossians 4:3*

CHRISTIAN RETAIL STORES CONTINUE to sustain a viable presence in the Christian book marketplace. While some industry veterans are concerned that more and more sales of Christian products are being taken over by Internet book sales and big-box discount competitors like Wal-Mart® and Target®, Christian retail stores continue to hold a large share of the sale of Christian products. While almost 350 Christian retail stores closed in 2005, 437 new Christian retail store locations opened in the same year. The net difference is a positive growth for the number of Christian retail stores. One CBA survey showed that well over half of all Christian stores expect to see an increase in sales and profits in 2006.

Research shows that an unbeliever must have seven to twelve significant contacts with the gospel message before they will become a Christian. This same principle holds true in marketing. Consumers generally need to be exposed to a new product seven to twelve times before they will purchase it. Familiarity is important.

The more consumers see and hear about a product, the more likely they will eventually purchase the product. This theory holds true in marketing books to the Christian marketplace. Exposure is essential. The more retailers see and hear about your books the more likely they are to place orders for your titles.

To effectively reach the Christian retail market, your books must be easily available for retailers to order. This means that your books should be available through at least one of the major Christian distributors or wholesale book companies (listed in Chapter 2, Secure Distribution). Christian retailers are busy. They do not want to open small accounts with many different sources. Most Christian retailers order from a handful of sources for ease in accounting as well as reduced shipping fees because many of the larger distribution and wholesale companies offer free shipping with larger orders. Furthermore, having your books available through established distribution channels signals retailers that you are serious about marketing your books.

This chapter will look at the most common and effective means to let Christian booksellers know about your books.

Industry Tradeshows

Industry tradeshows are designed to let Christian booksellers know about new products while giving them an opportunity to get information on the latest trends and technology affecting their business. Publishers and other suppliers for the Christian retail marketplace exhibit their new products at these shows. Industry tradeshows are mainly attended by Christian booksellers looking to acquire new products for their bookstores. The major Christian retail tradeshows are listed here.

- **International Christian Retail Show (ICRS)**

    ICRS is the largest Christian retail industry tradeshow. Held annually in July, the show draws attendees from all over the world looking to acquire Christian products. Sponsored by CBA, show exhibitors and attendees receive a discounted rate if they are members of CBA. Non-CBA member exhibitors must be approved by CBA prior to securing exhibit space. To exhibit at ICRS, publishers must demonstrate that a minimum of 10 Christian bookstores carry their products (preferably CBA member stores).

    www.cbaonline.org

- **CBA Advance/Expo**

    Also hosted by CBA, CBA Advance is a smaller version of ICRS held in winter each year. CBA Advance is a training conference for Christian retailers. The conference features Expo which is the exhibit hall for publishers and industry suppliers to promote their newest offerings to the retailers attending the conference.

    www.cbaonline.org

- **RBTE**

    RBTE stands for Religious Booksellers Trade Expo. This show is held annually around Memorial Day in Illinois. It is a gathering of the religious marketplace for Catholic, Episcopal, and other liturgical traditions. The Association of Catholic Booksellers and the Episcopal Booksellers Association hold their annual meetings at this tradeshow. This show is very accessible for small publishers as they allow some booth sharing.

    www.rbte.net

- **Christian Product Expo (CPE)**

    CPE is sponsored by the Munce Group for their member stores. The show is held each September in Nashville. It is a table-top show, meaning that the displays are centered on the products rather than around impressive signs and booth designs. This show is exclusively for Munce member retail stores and Munce pays for its member stores to attend the show if they write a minimum number of orders at the show.
    www.munce.com

- **CPE Regionals**

    Historically, ECPA (Evangelical Christian Publishers Association) held regional tradeshows for Christian retailers around the country in January each year. These shows were regionally based so that retailers who might not travel a long distance to a CBA show would still have an opportunity to attend a tradeshow and gather information on the latest Christian products and trends.

    Citing a steady drop in attendance and sales, ECPA announced that 2006 would be the last year that the organization would hold regional tradeshows. These regional tradeshows will be picked up by the Munce Group in January 2007. Munce will host two regional tradeshows (West Coast and East Coast) in 2007. They will add a third regional tradeshow in the Southeast in 2008. These tradeshows will run similarly to their annual CPE show, except that these shows will be open to all Christian retailers and suppliers.
    www.munce.com

- **Catholic Marketing Network Tradeshows**

    Catholic Marketing Network (CMN) sponsors two tradeshows annually: CMN Winter Tradeshow and CMN

International Tradeshow. These tradeshows are largely attended by Catholic book and gift stores, Catholic distributors, and Catholic media personnel. Only members of Catholic Marketing Network may exhibit at the tradeshow. Catholic Marketing Network retail members attend the tradeshows free of charge. These shows are accessible for small publishers as CMN does allow booth sharing.
www.catholicmarketing.com

- **The Gathering of Church Bookstores**
  Hosted annually by *The Church Bookstore* magazine (produced by Strang Communications), The Gathering of Church Bookstores is a conference for church bookstores. The conference features an exhibit hall where publishers can exhibit their products.
  www.thechurchbookstore.com

- **Charisma Book Expo**
  This brand new tradeshow will hold its inaugural show in September 2006 in Atlanta, Georgia. Hosted by Strang Communications, the publishers of *Charisma* magazine, this tradeshow's focus is on charismatic and Pentecostal materials. The first show will be open to both Christian retailers and the general public.
  www.charismabookexpo.com

In addition to bringing plenty of promotional materials (brochures, fliers, order forms) to a tradeshow, publishers exhibiting books should also plan to bring extra copies of the books they are displaying to give away as promotional titles. Providing free promotional copies of your books to media personnel, book reviewers, and chain bookstore buyers at tradeshows is a sharp marketing tool. Sometimes also having a "useful" promotional item to freely give to show attendees can generate long-term exposure to your products. Giving away bookmarks, pens, pencils, or even magnets with your book and contact information printed on them will remind those individuals of your books on an ongoing basis and can result in additional sales.

Holding author book signings at tradeshows is another good tool to bring Christian retail buyers' attention to your books. The majority of publishers host at least one author book signing for a new title at tradeshows. Books signed by an author at tradeshows are provided free of charge to retailers and other show attendees as author book signings are a promotional tool used to generate orders for the book from Christian retail stores.

Tradeshows used to be the major forum through which bookstores placed orders for books. As more publishers have increased their use of sales representatives to sell books directly to bookstores, tradeshows are no longer the main avenue through which booksellers order product. However, attendance at tradeshows is still important for establishing a presence in the Christian marketplace and for forming relationships within the industry. New publishers can gain recognition and acceptance in the industry through creating a presence at tradeshows.

Advertisements in Trade Journals

Publishers and suppliers can advertise their products to Christian retailers through trade journals aimed at Christian retailers. These journals give publishers another avenue to make their titles known to Christian retailers while encouraging them to stock the books in their stores.

Magazine advertisements do sell products. Look in any magazine and you will see that it is filled with advertisements. When you consider how vast the magazine industry is in America, it is evident that magazine advertisements work. If they did not, advertisements would not be driving the magazine industry and keeping magazines cost-effective for consumers. Remember, repetition is essential for selling with magazine advertisements.

Publishers have a few choices for advertising their books via trade journals to the Christian retail marketplace.

- *Aspiring Retail*

    The official magazine of CBA, *Aspiring Retail* is mailed free to all CBA members. Non-CBA members can pay for a subscription to the magazine. It is the only magazine in the industry written by retailers for retailers.

    Advertising is handled by Carlton Dunn and Associates.

    Carlton Dunn and Associates
    856-582-0690
    carl@carldunn.com
    www.carldunn.com

- *Christian Retailing*

    Produced by Strang Communications, *Christian Retailing* is mailed free of charge to any retail bookstore in America that is actively selling Christian products. Subscriptions can be ordered by individuals and industry suppliers.

    Advertising information can be found on Strang's website. www.strang.com/mediacentral.

    Strang Communications
    407-333-0600

- **The Church Bookstore**

   This publication, launched in 2004 by Strang Communications, is mailed six times each year, *The Church Bookstore* is geared for bookstores within churches. Church bookstores are currently the fastest growing segment of the Christian retail industry with some estimates placing the number of churches offering retail sales on Sundays at 30,000.

   Advertising information and contacts can be found on the magazine's website.
   www.thechurchbookstore.com

   The Church Bookstore
   407-333-7110

- **CMN *Trade Journal* / Seasonal Catalogs**

   Produced by Catholic Marketing Network and mailed free of charge to all CMN's member retail stores, the *CMN Trade Journal* is produced twice yearly. CMN also produces two seasonal catalogs yearly, offering their member Catholic retail stores a look at the latest products for the Catholic marketplace. Publishers do not need to be a member of CMN to advertise in the CMN Trade Journal or the seasonal catalogs.

   Advertising information and rates can be found on CMN's website.
   www.catholicmarketing.com

- ***BookWire Christian Publishing News & Reviews***

   This new quarterly publication, a joint venture of Evangelical Christian Publishers Association (ECPA) and R.R. Bowker, LLC, is set to launch in September 2006. Mailed free of charge to over 12,000 book professionals including general market librarians and book buyers, the publication features book reviews, book excerpts, interviews from Christian authors, and Christian publishing industry news. This publication is supported through Christian publishers advertising their products.

Contact:
- Josephine Murphy at josephine.murphy@bowker.com for advertising information and rates

R.R. Bowker
888-269-5372
www.bookwire.com

Advertisements in Wholesaler and Distributor Catalogs

Christian book wholesale companies and distributors produce catalogs that they distribute to Christian retail stores. Advertising in catalogs offered by those wholesale and distributor companies that carry your books is another marketing tool to reach Christian retail stores.

Promotional Opportunities Through Retail Marketing Groups

Many independent Christian retail stores are finding that they are unable to succeed in the marketplace as stand-alone stores. Retail marketing groups provide these stores the support they need in networking and marketing to remain viable in the current marketplace. Among their services, marketing groups offer their member stores marketing materials to hand out and/or mail to existing and potential customers. The majority of the cost of these materials is paid for by publishers' placing advertisements for products in these promotional materials. Member retail stores then pay a small fee to purchase the materials for their use with customers.

Advertising in retail marketing groups' promotional materials is an excellent use of advertising dollars. Retail marketing groups' catalogs fetch maximum exposure for your advertising dollar as they allow you to promote your titles to retail stores and consumers at the same time. Member retail stores are generally required to stock the items from the catalogs they are distributing to their customers. This policy ensures that stores will carry your books when you advertise through this venue. One requirement for advertising in these retail marketing catalogs is that you must have your titles available through at least one of the three wholesale companies serving the Christian retail marketplace (Spring Arbor, Appalachian, or Anchor).

Currently, four retail marketing groups provide opportunities for you to purchase advertisements in their promotional materials.

- **Covenant Group**

    Covenant Group is an association of leading Christian retailers. It is run by retailers and operates for the benefit of its eighty member Christian retail stores. They offer four seasonal catalogs and an annual church supplies catalog plus additional flyers to their member stores.

    Contact:
    - Dianne Yon at DYon@CovenantGrp.net for information on advertising with Covenant Group

Covenant Group
P.O. Box 170129
1600 John B. White Blvd. - Suite 1003
Spartanburg, SC 29301
864-587-2637
www.covenantgroupstores.com

- **Munce Group**

The Munce Group claims to be the nation's largest Christian full-service marketing group. Sporting nearly 600 Christian retail members, the Munce Group offers 15 different catalogs and multiple flyers for their member stores. Member stores are required to at least participate in the spring and Christmas catalogs. Most member retailers participate in four to six promotions each year. These catalogs reach millions of consumers.

Contact:
- Sue Brewer at sue.brewer@munce.com for information on advertising with the Munce Group

Munce Group
415 Second St.
Indian Rocks Beach, FL 33785
727-596-7625
www.munce.com

- **Parable™ Group**

Similar to the Munce Group, the over 300 member stores of the Parable group maintain their independent identity while receiving full-service marketing support. Parable offers its member stores nearly 30 promotional publications throughout the year. Member stores are required to participate in Parable's two flagship catalogs each year (spring and Christmas) and are required to carry reasonable stock of any products featured in the catalogs they are participating in. To have your products considered for any of the Parable promotions, contact the merchandiser who handles the product line for your materials.

Contact:
- David McShea at dave.mcshea@parable.com for books, Bibles, and software
- Sally Stevenson at sally.stevenson@parable.com for children's product
- Val Lund at val.lund@parable.com for gifts and exclusives

Parable Group
805-543-2644
www.parablegroup.com

- **Logos Bookstore Association**

A group of independently owned and operated Christian bookstores in the United States and Canada, Logos Bookstore Association is the smallest of the retail marketing groups. The 30 member stores in this association carry a core of product in common but each store also has the ability to reflect the needs of its community in choice of additional products. The Logos Bookstore Association produces spring and Christmas catalogs for their member stores.

Logos Bookstore Association offers publishers two additional ways to tell its member stores about your products. Logos publishes a monthly newsletter ten times each year (no July or December issues). Logos will mail your sample, catalog, or flier with their newsletter to member stores at no cost to you. All you need to do is mail to Logos Bookstore Association enough copies of your materials for the Logos member stores. Logos must receive your materials prior to the 15th of the month you want the materials sent to their member stores. Logos also publishes a Hot Tips email for its member stores every Wednesday. This email contains news, prayer requests, and vendor specials.

Contact:
- Becky Gorczyca at becky@logosbookstores.com for advertising in Logos catalogs
- Submit information on product specials for the Hot Tips email by fax to 330-677-8049

Logos Bookstore Association
1949 State Route 59 Suite 203
Kent, OH 44240
330-677-8086
www.logosbookstores.com

Christian Booksellers Association Consumer Catalogs

Four booksellers associations serve Christian retailers: CBA, The Association of Catholic Booksellers, Episcopal Booksellers Association, and Christian African American Booksellers Association. CBA is the largest and all-encompassing of these associations. It serves all Christian bookstores from Catholic to Episcopal to Evangelical and includes booksellers reaching the

African American Christian marketplace. The other three booksellers associations are much smaller and serve retail stores geared toward a specific market within the Christian marketplace.

- **The Association of Catholic Booksellers**

    This association is made up of 40 independent Catholic bookstores across the United States and Canada. Catholic Booksellers hosts a catalog partnership program for their member bookstores. The catalog, *Catholic Gifts & Books*, is published annually in the fall. Publishers pay to advertise in the catalog and participating stores purchase the catalog to mail to their customers. The catalog's main focus is gifts with a few pages dedicated to books.

    The association holds its annual meeting at RBTE each year. They provide their member stores with a quarterly e-newsletter and special mailings from publishers on new titles, specials, and promotions.

    Contact:
    - Dan Pierson at danpierson@catholicbooksellers.org for a vendor submission kit for *Catholic Gifts & Books*

    Daniel J. Pierson, Director
    The Association of Catholic Booksellers
    491 Prestwick Dr. SE
    Grand Rapids, MI 49546
    616-956-5044
    www.catholicbooksellers.org

- **Christian African American Booksellers Association (CAABA)**

    This organization grew out of African American Christian booksellers' needs to share common problems, learn methods to effectively operate their stores, and increase awareness about the limited product offerings available to their predominantly African American customers. CAABA provides its member retail stores with a quarterly newsletter, *CAABA Chronicle*, as well as catalogs and special mailings, which stores can use to promote products to customers and potential customers throughout the year. Publishers and authors can advertise to the African American Christian retail community through these catalogs, special mailings, and newsletter.

    The Munce group produces CAABA's catalogs. Advertising discounts are provided for CAABA member publishers and authors.

    CAABA
    P.O. Box 512053
    Los Angeles, CA 90051
    323-751-7323
    caabamail@aol.com
    www.caaba.net

- **Episcopal Booksellers Association, Inc.**

    The Episcopal Booksellers Association is made up of 80 Episcopal bookstores across the United States and Canada. This association hosts a catalog partnership program for Episcopal bookstores and publishers. The catalog is produced annually in the fall. Publishers pay a fee to place a title in the catalog, and participating Episcopal stores (about a quarter of the member stores) purchase copies of the catalog to mail to their customers. The interior of the catalog is uniform while each bookstore is able to customize the cover for their particular store. This is a book catalog. Over 90% of the products listed in the catalog are book titles.

This association holds its annual meeting at RBTE each year. It hosts a supporting vendor membership, which provides publishers this identification when marketing books to Episcopal bookstores.

Contact:
- Nancy Marshall at nancy@episcopalbookstore.com for publisher submission guidelines and deadlines for the Episcopal Bookstore Partnership Catalog

Henrietta Speaks, Executive Director
Episcopal Booksellers Association
EBAxxutivDIR@aol.com
www.episcopalbooksellers.org

- **Catholic Book Publishers Association (CBPA)**

CBPA, while not a bookseller's association (it is a publishers association), offers a consumer catalog, *The Spirit of Books*, which is published twice yearly. These catalogs are distributed through Catholic bookstores. The Catholic bookstores in turn mail the catalogs to their own customer lists and use them as in-store promotional pieces. Only current publisher members of the CBPA are eligible to advertise titles in these catalogs. Advertising information is available on CBPA's website.

www.cbpa.org

Direct Mail Campaigns

A direct mail or email campaign to reach Christian retail stores is another marketing option. However, direct mail campaigns tend not to be as successful as advertising in trade journals or consumer catalogs for retail store use. With over 24,000 Christian books published each year, booksellers are overwhelmed with choices of what to carry in their stores. The typical Christian retailer buys from 35 to 40 publishers. As a result, unsolicited mail or email that comes across a book buyer's desk generally receives the least amount of attention.

The average response rate on direct mail marketing is one to two percent of your mailing. However, if you have a unique marketing angle or a book by a known Christian personality, the response rate from direct mail can be higher than the average. Three main organizations offer rental mailing lists for Christian retail stores.

- **CBA (Christian Booksellers Association)**

    CBA offers four different U.S. Christian retail mailing lists: CBA Premium List, CBA Member Stores List, Non-member Stores List, and Combined CBA Member / Non-member List. The Premium list provides 1,000 addresses of Christian chain store headquarters and the largest independent CBA stores. The CBA Member Stores List is just that; it contains 1,900 addresses of CBA's member stores. The Non-member Stores List is a listing of 7,600 non-member Christian retail businesses including in-church stores and college bookstores. The Combined List provides 9,500 addresses.

    CBA offers these rental mailing lists in three different formats: adhesive labels, on disk, or via email. Rates vary for each list. CBA also offers these same lists in a database format for publishers who want to use the addresses repeatedly for mailing. Of course, the price for the database is much higher than for the list rental.

> CBA
> P.O. Box 62000
> Colorado Springs, CO 80962-2000
> 800-858-1950
> www.cbaonline.org

- **Strang Communications**

Strang Communications, the publisher of both the *Christian Retailing* magazine and *The Church Bookstore* magazine, also offers rental mailing lists of Christian retail stores. At this time, they do not offer mailing lists for church bookstores, but plan to make that available sometime in 2007.

> David Manning, List Rental Manager
> David.manning@strang.com
> 407-333-7138
> www.strang.com

- **Catholic Book Publishers Association (CBPA)**

CBPA maintains a mailing list of approximately 1,400 Catholic bookstores. The list is available on a one-time rental basis. It comes already printed on labels or on a diskette. Members of CBPA receive a discounted rate for the mailing list.

- CBPA members contact:
  CBPA
  815-332-3245
  cbpa3@aol.com
  www.cbpa.org

- Non-members contact:
  Catholic Church / School Market
  43 Zurich Way
  Tell City, IN 47586
  812-547-8516

Direct Sales

Sales representatives making personal sales calls to bookstore buyers is one of the most effective sales techniques in selling books to retail stores. However, most small and self-publishers cannot afford sales representatives to traverse the country and make personal calls to Christian bookstore buyers. Apart from national sales representation, small publishers should at least make sales calls to those chain bookstores with buyers headquartered in your locale as well as the larger independent bookstores located in your corner of the country.

For a listing of member CBA Christian stores in your state, visit http://cba.know-where.com/cba.

Most of the largest Christian retail chain stores will review new products from small publishers to determine if these products fit into their current product mix. These chain stores allow small publishers to submit new products for review. When submitting products for review to a chain bookstores headquarters, you should include your marketing plans, book reviews garnered, and the distributors that carry your books. Most chains will not consider a submitted product that is not available through Spring Arbor or Appalachian Distributors.

Following is a listing of the major Christian chain bookstores.

- **Berean® Christian Stores**

    Berean operates 17 stores. Many of their stores are among the largest Christian retail stores in the United States. Product submission guidelines can be found on their website.

    Berean Christian Stores
    Merchandise Submission Department
    8121 Hamilton Ave
    Cincinnati, OH 45231
    www.berean.com

- **Cokesbury Bookstores**

    Cokesbury is the retail division of the United Methodist Publishing House. It operates 71 retail stores across the United States. Cokesbury carries a core inventory of product for all its retail stores, but individual retail store managers also have authority to order additional products they feel would fit with their individual consumer base. To submit product for review to Cokesbury, contact their headquarters first to determine the category buyer to which your books should be sent.

    Cokesbury Bookstores
    201 Eighth Ave. S.
    P.O. Box 801
    Nashville, TN 37202
    615-749-6000
    www.cokesbury.com

- **Family® Christian Stores**

    Family Christian Stores is the largest chain of Christian bookstores in the United States. They operate 320 stores. Product submission guidelines can be found on their website.

    Family Christian Stores
    Attn: General Merchandise / A-5
    5300 Patterson Ave. SE
    Grand Rapids, MI 49530
    www.familychristian.com

- **Lemstone® Christian Stores**

    Lemstone, LLC, operates 34 franchise Christian retail stores. To submit product for review to Lemstone, contact their headquarters first to determine which buyer your product should be sent to.

    Lemstone Christian Stores
    A Division of Lemstone, LLC.
    1749 South Naperville Road; Suite 200
    Wheaton, IL 60187
    630-682-1400
    www.lemstone.com

- **Lifeway® Christian Stores**

    Lifeway Christian Resources of the Southern Baptist Convention owns and operates 125 Lifeway Christian Stores throughout the United States. Lifeway produces a consumer catalog that their member stores utilize as a marketing tool. Small publishers can advertise their products in this catalog. Products that are advertised in the catalog are carried by the Lifeway Christian Stores. Information on advertising in the

Lifeway catalog and contact information can be found on their website.

Lifeway Christian Stores
One Lifeway Plaza
Nashville, TN 37234
www.lifeway.com

- **Mardel Christian and Educational Supply**

    Mardel operates 21 stores. To submit product for review to Mardel, contact their headquarters first to determine which buyer to send your books to.

    Mardel Christian and Educational Supply
    7727 SW 44th St.
    Oklahoma City, OK 73179
    405-745-1300
    www.mardel.com

Summary

Sales through Christian bookstores account for about 56% of Christian book sales. Keeping Christian retail a viable entity benefits all publishers publishing materials for the Christian marketplace since Christian bookstores carry the largest selection of Christian materials of any retail outlet. While the majority of a Christian small publisher's book sales may not come directly through Christian retail stores, this market is still an important avenue in making your books available to Christian consumers. A number of Christian consumers are loyal to their local Christian bookstore. When these individuals hear about a new book, they prefer to purchase the book through their local Christian bookstore. A marketing campaign that includes Christian retail stores can serve to bring additional sales for your books.

Connect with Churches 7

Preach the Word; be prepared in season and out of season; correct, rebuke and encourage—with great patience and careful instruction.
—2 Timothy 4:2

HUNDREDS OF THOUSANDS OF CHURCHES exist in the United States representing over 1,000 different church denominations, most of which can be sorted into 15 main denominational families based on their historical roots. Currently, the denominational families with the most members are Catholic, Baptist, Methodist/Wesleyan, Lutheran, Presbyterian, Pentecostal/Charismatic, and Episcopalian/Anglican. These churches, collectively, have thousands more leaders providing leadership for their congregations.

Each church in America represents numerous Christian consumers. In a 2002 survey, the Pew Research Council found that 52% of the population in the United States identified themselves as Protestant (154 million) and 24% identified themselves as Catholic (71 million). Churches provide a number of different opportunities for you to promote your books to Christian readers.

Church Libraries

While the trend for many newer Christian churches is to offer retail Christian book sales, church libraries still remain a prominent avenue for book sales. The majority of churches across America host a church library. Conservative estimates place church libraries at 50,000 across the United States. These libraries can be as small as a single bookshelf or as large as an entire room in a church. Most have a designated librarian who is in charge of library maintenance and purchasing of materials.

One effective method for marketing to a large number of church libraries is through a church library association. Most church library associations hold an annual convention for their members. These conventions provide publishers opportunities to exhibit your book and/or place promotional inserts in the convention program packets for reasonable fees. Church library associations also publish regular newsletters or journals for their members. These newsletters print reviews of Christian products and some include paid advertisements, providing more avenues for you to promote your titles.

Some of these associations also provide mailing list rentals of their member libraries. You can use these lists to conduct a target mailing to further promote your books to church libraries.

The primary church library associations are listed here.

- **Catholic Library Association (CLA)**
  CLA is an international organization for Catholic church and school libraries. Their quarterly publication, *Catholic Library World*, features book reviews and advertising. CLA's annual convention is held in conjunction with the National Catholic Education Association's (NCEA) annual convention.
  www.cathla.org

- **Church and Synagogue Library Association (CSLA)**
    CSLA publishes their own bi-monthly publication, *Church & Synagogue LIBRARIES*. This publication features reviews of new materials. CSLA also holds an annual national conference.
    http://cslainfo.org

- **The Evangelical Church Library Association (ECLA)**
    ECLA is a national library association for church and Christian school librarians. They produce a quarterly publication, *Church Libraries*, which features advertisements and dedicates about 75% of its material to reviews of products. ECLA hosts a convention in Wheaton, Illinois each year.
    www.eclalibraries.org

- **National Church Library Association (NCLA)**
    Formerly Lutheran Church Library Association, NCLA now serves Christian church libraries of all denominations. NCLA hosts a national conference and publishes *Libraries Alive*, a quarterly publication featuring advertisements and reviews of books.
    www.churchlibraries.org

- **Pacific Northwest Association of Church Libraries (PNACL)**
    PNACL is a regional association for church libraries in the Pacific Northwest (Washington, Oregon, and Idaho). They host an annual conference and a quarterly newsletter, *The Lamplighter*, which features reviews of books.
    www.pnacl.org

A fairly complete list of congregational library associations can be found online at http://web.nmsu.edu/~ebosman/church/libassoc.shtml.

Church Leaders

Church leaders tend to read Christian books. A study by the Barna Group found that although the typical Protestant pastor makes less than the average household income, these pastors rank among the top 10% of book buyers in America. Almost all of these pastors (98%) had purchased at least one book in the last year and the typical pastor bought 20 volumes in that time frame. One out of every five pastors purchased 50 or more titles in one year, an average of about one book per week!

Church leaders are influential. Senior pastors, associate pastors, youth pastors, children's ministers, Sunday school teachers, small group Bible study leaders, and women's ministry leaders are all individuals within a church who hold the authority to recommend books to church attendees. Surveys show that many people take the recommendations of their church leaders when it comes to what books to read and buy. Generally, if a pastor recommends something from the pulpit, people buy it. Even Sunday school teachers' and small group leaders' recommendations are powerful in motivating people to purchase and read books.

A number of avenues are available to promote books to these church leaders.

1. Church Denominations

For authors or publishers who are strongly aligned with a church denomination, a good marketing strategy is to promote your titles through your denomination. Church denominations have many avenues for you to promote titles. Most denominations have national and regional conferences for their various church leaders. Many have regular publications that feature advertisements, announcements, and even product reviews that are sent to member churches. Some denominations host their own web-based bookstore for their member churches' leaders and members. Member church directories or mailing lists can often be obtained from the denominational headquarters for direct mailings. Also, making personal contact with the denominational head of the department within the church you are trying to reach (i.e., Women's Ministries, Children's Ministries, Youth Pastors, etc.) could garner a promotion of your book within that department of the denomination.

The best way to find which opportunities exist to promote your titles through any church denomination is to visit the denomination's main website. Since there are too many church denominations to feature adequately here (a whole book could be devoted just for church denominations), below is a sampling of two church denominations with some of the promotional opportunities they provide.

- **Presbyterian Church in America (PCA)**

    PCA holds an annual national assembly for church leaders and members featuring an exhibit hall. Their Christian Education and Publications division hosts a "Women in the Church Leadership Training Conference" for women who want to be lay leaders in the church. They also hold an annual Children's Ministry Conference. This division also features an online Christian education and publications bookstore for church leaders. An online directory of member churches by state and a print version of their member church directory are also available. PCA's Christian Education and Publications division has its own website separate from the main PCA website. The Christian Education and Publication division's website is **www.pcacep.org**.
    www.pcanet.org

- **Free Methodist Church**

    The Free Methodist Church holds annual regional conferences for their church leaders. They produce *Light & Life*, a bi-monthly magazine with a circulation of 55,000 (mostly to Free Methodist church members), featuring articles and advertisements. The denomination's website features reviews of books of interest to pastors. An international women's ministry featuring an annual conference and regular newsletter is also part of the denomination. The church's website hosts an online directory of member churches by state.
    www.freemethodistchurch.org

2. Church Leaders' Conferences

There are a number of national and regional church leadership conferences that are not denomination specific. These conferences draw from a wide range of churches. Conferences exist for pastors, youth pastors, and Christian education leaders. Many opportunities exist within these conferences to reach church leaders. Publishers can exhibit products or place promotional materials in the conference packets that are handed out to conference attendees. Some conferences allow advertising in their conference programs and others allow publishers to have authors speak on their books' topics in a seminar. Below is a listing of various nondenominational church conferences. It is by no means a comprehensive list, but a sampling of what is available for marketing books to church leaders.

- **Pastor Conferences**

    If you have a book a church pastor would be interested in, consider this type of conference to reach pastors with your product. Remember, if a pastor likes a book and recommends it to his congregation, church members will purchase and read it. Three examples of national conferences geared toward pastors are The National Conference for Catechetical Leadership at www.nccl.org, the National Pastor's Convention at www.nationalpastors.com, and the National Outreach Convention at www.outreachmediagroup.com.

- **Youth Pastor Conferences**

    For books geared toward teenagers, connecting with youth pastors is a good way to get your book in the hands of teens. Youth pastors often recommend good books to their youth groups. Youth Specialties at www.youthspecialties.com/NYWC hosts National Youth Workers Conventions regionally around the country. Youth Source Ministries at www.nylc.net holds a National Youth Leader Conference on both the East Coast and West Coast. The National Federation for Catholic Youth Ministries at http://www.nfcym.org/ncyc also holds an annual conference for Catholic youth and youth leaders.

- **Children's Pastor Conferences**

    Churches stock their Sunday school and child care rooms with resources for the children and teachers. These resources include books for the children to look at and read. Marketing to children's pastors can result in churches' ordering your products for their children's rooms. Parents, in turn, are exposed to the books and may decide to purchase them for their children. Children's pastors also often recommend good books to parents for educating their children in the faith.

    One good way to reach a large number of children's pastors is through a conference for this group. The Network of Children's Ministry at www.incm.org holds annual International Children's Pastors Conferences at three locations around the United States.

- **Christian Education Conferences**

    Most nondenominational Christian education conferences geared toward adult and children's ministry leaders are held in regional or state locations in the spring. Many Christian education conferences tend to be small, drawing just from their surrounding area. Some of these conferences are regional in scope and boast higher attendances. These include:
    - Chicagoland Church Ministries Convention at www.gcssa.org in Illinois
    - Northwest Christian Education Conference at www.nwcec.org in Washington State
    - Bass Church Workers Convention at www.bassconvention.org in California
    - Mid-Atlantic Christian Education Conference at www.macea.org in North Carolina
    - Religious Education Congress at www.recongress.org in California

3. Direct Mail

One technique to gain the attention of church leaders for your titles is to generate your own postcard, flier, or brochure and conduct a direct mailing. Church mailing lists can be obtained from various organizations. Many church mailing lists can be ordered according to denomination, church size, ethnic churches, or by church ministry. Some companies providing church mailing lists offer an introductory rate for new users to test market a portion of a mailing list. Three good sources for church mailing lists are Outreach Media Group at www.outreachmediagroup.com, American Church Lists at www.americanchurchlists.com, and The Official Catholic Directory at www.officialcatholicdirectory.com.

A direct mail campaign can be costly. A cheaper direct mail option for promoting your titles to church leaders is advertising in a card pack. Direct mailing service companies print promotional cards for businesses and then mail packets containing these cards to pastors and churches. Card packs can be much more cost effective than direct mail. Research figures indicate that advertising in a card pack can cost up to 75% less than a solo direct mailing. Many promotional card pack services also offer introductory rates so that advertisers can test the market. Three companies that offer promotional mailing packets for churches and church leaders are Tri-Media Marketing Services at www.trimediaonline.com, National Response Marketing, Inc. at www.nrm-inc.com, and the Outreach Media Group at www.outreachmediagroup.com.

4. Advertising in Magazines and Journals

Placing advertisements in magazines and journals that target various church leaders can enhance your marketing campaign to churches. A better option is to get free coverage through submitting an article to a magazine or journal that provides church leaders with useful information. Using an excerpt from the book you wish to promote is one great way to gain church leaders' attention for your title.

The Christian Writer's Market Guide by Sally E. Stuart is an invaluable resource for locating magazines and journals targeted to various church leaders. Sally E. Stuart's book features both topical and target market alphabetical listings of periodicals and e-zines for the Christian marketplace and includes publications specifically geared for church leaders. A listing of Christian magazines and journals can also be found on Sally E. Stuart's helpful website at www.stuartmarket.com/Magazines.html.

Bible Schools and Seminaries

Publishers with theological books may want to consider marketing to religious studies professors and bookstores at seminaries and Bible schools. Two main associations serve this market and provide resources for reaching this unique group.

- **Association of Theological Booksellers (ATB)**

    ATB is an association of academic theological bookstores for seminaries and Bible schools. This organization produces a book catalog, *Theological Best Books*, twice yearly in the spring and fall. The spring edition features new and bestselling titles in Pastoral Ministry and Spirituality while the fall edition features new and bestselling titles in Theology, Biblical Studies, History, Contemporary Issues, and Reference. These catalogs are shipped in bulk to seminary and theological center bookstores for distribution to students, seminarians, faculty, alumni, and other customers. The catalogs are also mailed to members of the American Academy of Religion and to subscribers of the *Journal of Pastoral Care*. ATB also rents mailing lists for seminary and Bible school academic bookstores.

    Association of Theological Booksellers
    Charles A. Roth
    P.O. Box 96
    Sea Cliff, NY 11579
    516-674-8603
    charles@rothadvertising.com
    http://associationoftheologicalbooksellers.org

- **American Academy of Religion (AAR)**

    AAR is the world's largest association of academics who research or teach topics related to religion. AAR is a "religious" organization rather than a "Christian" organization in that the Academy does not endorse or reject any religious tradition or set of religious beliefs or practices. However, many Christian academic scholars are members of this academy. The AAR publishes four publications that accept advertisements. They also hold an annual meeting each year. The annual meeting of the AAR has opportunities for publishers to exhibit their books as well as advertise in the meeting's program. This organization also has a mailing list of their members which can be rented.

    American Academy of Religion
    825 Houston Mill Rd. NE, Ste. 300
    Atlanta, GA 30329
    404-727-3049
    aar@aarweb.org
    www.aarweb.org

Creative Marketing

Innovative thinking can lead to effective marketing in reaching church leaders with your books. For example, if you are a publisher in the Seattle area, consider The Church Council of Greater Seattle at www.churchcouncilseattle.org, which has neighborhood clergy groups that meet regularly to support each other and discuss areas of concern. One idea would be to make promotional copies of your book available to the pastors at one or more of these neighborhood clergy groups at their regular meeting.

Another example for publishers in Illinois is Deer Ridge Ministries at www.deerridgeministries.org. This ministry provides pastors and their wives free week-long retreat stays to rest body and soul. A creative marketing idea would be to make gift copies of a book you have published (one that could be an encouragement resource for pastors or their wives) available to the pastoral couples using the retreat. Whenever you make promotional copies available free of charge in this manner, include a letter with the book that tells the recipient that this copy of the book is a gift from you. Also include information on how to order additional copies and on how to book the author for a speaking engagement.

Access Christian Consumers 8

*But encourage one another daily, as long as it is called Today,
so that none of you may be hardened by sin's deceitfulness.*
—*Hebrews 3:13*

CHRISTIAN CONSUMERS ABOUND in the United States. The most recent census figures place the population of the United States at 296.4 million people. Surveys indicate that about 76 percent of these individuals identify themselves as Christian. That means that there are potentially over 225 million Christian consumers to whom you could market your books.

In 2003, the Barna Group reported that half of all adults and teenagers in the United States reported reading at least one Christian book other than the Bible in the last year. One third of adults and teenagers in the United States also reported purchasing a Christian book (other than the Bible) in the same time period. Surprisingly, the Barna Group also found that many people not connected to the Christian faith indicated that they had read at least one Christian book (other than the Bible) in the past year.

In 2005, ECPA released its "Christian Book and Consumer Report." This report showed that Christian book buyers read more and spend more on books than the average book buyer in America. Households that purchase Christian books spent $100 more per year on books than compared to the average book buying household. Interestingly, this study revealed that book recommendations happen more frequently among Christian readers than with any other reading population.

Christian consumers are readers. However, to succeed as a publisher in the Christian marketplace, you need to use every element you can to attract every Christian consumer who would benefit from or enjoy your books. A number of Christian channels provide multiple opportunities to draw the attention of Christian consumers to your books. Authors can help with this aspect of book promotion. There are a number of activities that authors can do to increase exposure (and thus sales) of their book to Christian consumers. Publishers are wise to discuss with their authors (prior to accepting a book for publication) what specific aspects of book promotion the authors are willing to be involved in. These promotional activities can be included in the book contract that is negotiated between the publisher and author.

Christian Magazines

Literally hundreds of Christian magazines exist. A Christian magazine can be found for every category you can think of: children, teenagers, young adults, men, women, fathers, mothers, grandparents, senior adults, pastors, teachers, musicians, writers, nurses, counselors, businessmen and women, marriage, money management, prayer, etc. The best resource for a comprehensive list of Christian periodicals is *Christian Writer's Market Guide* by Sally E. Stuart. This guide provides a listing of current Christian magazines and e-zines arranged both alphabetically by target market and by topical listing. Two other sources for lists of Christian magazines are online at www.stuartmarket.com/Magazines.html and www.findchristianmagazines.com.

Magazines provide you three main avenues to expose Christian consumers to your books.

1. Advertisements

As mentioned earlier, advertisements drive the magazine industry. The bulk of a magazine's income comes from advertisements. If magazine advertisements were not effective, this income source for the magazine industry would have dried up long ago. However, it is important to remember that a consumer generally needs to see an advertisement for a product seven to twelve times before purchasing the product. Therefore, when considering magazine advertisements, it is best to carefully select the magazines that target the category of Christians your book is geared toward and budget for repeat advertisements in these publications.

2. Articles

Many Christian magazines' articles come from freelance writers' submissions. Editorial calendars and guidelines for article submissions generally can be found on a publication's website or requested from the magazine editor via email. The majority of magazines also accept reprints (articles that have been printed in other publications) as long as the submission clearly states the article is a reprint and when and where it has been printed before.

Magazine articles are a powerful, free marketing tool for authors. Authors can submit articles based on the subject matter of their books or an excerpt from a book. Since most magazines accept secondary rights to material (meaning the material has been published elsewhere before), excerpts from books make great periodical articles. When these articles are accepted, your byline can list the title of the book providing publicity for your book. Readers who are interested in the subject matter of the article will then purchase the book to learn more. This same technique can be used for fiction stories. Many magazines feature fiction pieces and will run an excerpt of a fiction book. An additional boon from article submission for authors is that many publications provide payment for the articles they use.

Authors may need to get permission from their publisher prior to submitting book excerpts for publication. Some publishers' contracts specify that the publisher owns the book material while the book is in print. Generally, most publishers willing grant permission for authors to submit book excerpt articles as this helps with publicity.

Writing regular columns for magazines is another publicity option. Once you have published a few articles in a Christian magazine, you can approach that magazine's editor and suggest a regular column that you could write for the magazine. Columns are a good way to establish yourself as an expert in a subject, gather a loyal reader base, and generate ongoing exposure for your published books.

3. Book Reviews

A number of Christian magazines run reviews of books. However, most of these magazines do not have their own book reviewers. Rather, they accept book review articles from freelance writers. Again, Sally E. Stuart's *Christian Writer's Market Guide* indicates which publications print book reviews. It is advantageous for a publisher to form a mutually beneficial relationship with a freelance writer. In such a relationship, the freelance writer agrees to review the publisher's book(s) and submit book review articles on the book(s) to various Christian magazines. The publisher benefits from the publicity and the freelance writer benefits from the income derived from the articles. One advantage of magazines is that a book does not need to be brand-new for a publication to run a review. As long as the book is still relevant, the publication may decide to use the review.

Christian Newspapers

Over 250 Christian newspapers are published and distributed throughout the United States reaching a readership of millions of people. This is definitely a medium not to be overlooked in a publisher's marketing plans. The majority of Christian newspapers are regionally distributed with each publication having its own feel and local appeal. A few Christian newspapers, generally those that are denominationally based, are distributed nationally.

1. Marketing Opportunities

Most Christian newspapers are offered to readers free of charge. Thus these papers heavily rely on advertisers to provide the revenue needed to sustain their operation. Advertising in Christian newspapers is one means to access Christian consumers.

Christian newspapers offer other marketing opportunities beyond advertising. Some newspapers run Christian product reviews, while others print announcements about local Christians and Christian organizations, and most include a calendar of Christian events for their area. Publishers can make use of these opportunities in Christian newspapers to either have a product reviewed, submit a news release about an upcoming product, or place a notice in the paper's events calendar about an author's book signing at a local store. It is wise to target Christian newspapers in both the publisher's and the author's communities for press releases on new books, especially if the newspaper can feature the author in an article. If an author is undertaking a book signing tour, make sure to send press releases for both articles and events calendar to local Christian newspapers for each community in which your author will appear.

2. Associations

Christian newspapers are as plentiful and diverse as the Christian faith. While there is no central registry of Christian newspapers, there are a couple newspaper associations for Christian newspapers. Some of these associations list their members on their website while others provide a list of their members for a fee.

- **The Associated Church Press**

    This is the oldest religious press association in North America. This association's members are publishers of ecumenical or interfaith publications whose majority of readership is a Christian audience. Their membership list is sorted by faith affiliation as well as publisher type (newspaper, magazine, newsletter, or news website).
    www.theacp.org

- **The Catholic Press Association (CPA)**

    CPA lists all Diocesan newspapers by state. They also list all other national and regional Catholic newspapers that are members of CPA. CPA owns Catholic Advertising Network (CAN) which is an ad placement service for the Diocesan newspapers.
    www.catholicpress.org

- **Evangelical Press Association (EPA)**

    EPA exists to promote the cause of Evangelical Christianity and enhance the influence of Christian journalism. Their members include publishers of both newspapers and periodicals. A listing of their members with links to each website is available on EPA's website. They also rent their member list for a fee. Many of the church denominational newspapers are members of EPA.

    www.epassoc.org

3. Services

Ad placement services can be useful for placing advertisements in a large number of Christian newspapers to increase exposure of your books. As already mentioned, CPA hosts an ad placement service for their member newspapers. Another agency, Grace Christian Media (www.gracechristianmedia.com), also offers ad placement services for 260 Christian newspapers.

Press release services are another means to effectively reach a large number of newspapers. Generally press release services charge a fee to send a press release to a list of newspapers and journalists, but they provide no guarantee that the newspapers will print the information.

- **Grace Christian Media**

    This agency offers a press release service in addition to their ad placement service for over 100 Christian newspapers. For a fee they will send your press release to the publisher or editor of each newspaper.

    www.gracechristianmedia.com

- **Religion Press Release Services (RPRS)**
  RPRS distributes press releases to the subscribers of Religion News Service for a fee. Religion News Service subscribers include both secular and Christian newspapers.
  www.religionnews.com

4. Religion Coverage in General Newspapers

One other newspaper resource worth mentioning is the religion section in local general market newspapers. Most newspapers have a religion section at least once a week. Many of these religion sections carry articles on local figures in the religion community. Sending a press release to the religion editor of the local newspaper where the author of your newest title lives can result in coverage of that author and the new book. It is important to slant your press release in a manner that will grab the attention of the religion editor and give her some material to consider that is of interest to the newspaper's reading audience.

Authors should keep up-to-date on what news is being reported. Then when you notice press coverage around issues related to your book(s), use these news articles as opportunities to send out new press releases to newspaper editors announcing your book and how it ties into the current news. Reporters frequently need experts to quote and when you have written a book, you become an expert on that book's subject.

Publishers and authors can search on-line for general market newspapers in your locale and then submit press releases to the religion reporters. Two websites which list newspapers across the United States by state are www.onlinenewspapers.com and http://newslink.org. Another option is to utilize the advertising venues that the following organization provides to reach religion reporters.

- **Religion Newswriters Association (RNA)**

    This association is for print and broadcast reporters who cover religion in the general circulation news media. They have a few avenues available for publishers to reach their members with information on your latest books. RNA rents their mailing list of member reporters, they host an annual conference where publishers can exhibit or advertise, and they produce an annual calendar where publishers can alert reporters of a new title in the month it will be released.

    www.rna.org

Christian Radio and Television

Radio and television coverage is one of the most effective ways to reach a large number of Christian consumers and generate interest in a book. Interestingly, radio in the United States is a growing industry. The number of Christian radio and television stations in the United States is astounding. The Barna Group reports that nearly half of U.S. adults (46%) listen to a Christian radio broadcast in a typical month.

Some books lend themselves better to talk radio and television then others. Broader interest non-fiction adult Christian books on topics such as relationships, health, parenting, and the like are better candidates for radio and television exposure then many fiction or children's books. However, if a fiction or children's title has a unique angle that would be of interest to the general public it could be a candidate for radio or television. Acquiring radio and television interviews is difficult work and having a fascinating topic and a great pitch letter improves your chances of catching a producer's attention.

1. Publicity Services

The best way to access Christian radio and television stations is through publicity services. Publicity services vary depending on the amount of money you are willing to pay. The highest price service is engaging a publicist who will book guest appearances on radio and television programs for you. A lower price option is advertising in a publication that promotes radio and television media guests to producers. Your cheapest option is to use a press release service to send your press release to targeted media and pray that your release will engage a producer's interest.

- **National Religious Broadcasters (NRB)**

    The NRB is an association for Christian radio and television personnel. The association publishes a magazine nine times per year, which is the Christian broadcasting industry's premiere trade publication. Authors and publishers seeking guest interviews can advertise in this magazine. The NRB also hosts a national convention each year where publishers and authors can exhibit their materials to draw the attention of radio and television producers.
    www.nrb.org

- **Radio and Records (R&R)**

    R&R is an information company serving the key decision makers in the general market radio and record industry. They hosted an inaugural R&R Christian Summit in 2005 for the Christian radio and record communities and now plan to hold this summit annually. One savvy publisher chose to place a complimentary copy of a new book in each hotel room for this summit and garnered many Christian radio interviews from this promotion.

R&R also produces a weekly newspaper and e-newsletter for the radio and record industry (general market but includes Christian stations) that features books of interest to producers. Authors and publishers can send press releases or review copies of new titles for inclusion in the newspaper and e-newsletter. Advertising is also available for those seeking to generate more interest in acquiring interviews.
www.radioandrecords.com

- **Christian News Today (CNT)**
CNT has a newswire service which sends press releases to Christian radio and television show producers for a fee. This service also has a program for posting a press release on their website for a lower fee. Those seeking interviews can use this service to announce new titles and the availability of authors for guest interviews.
www.christiannewstoday.com

- **Christian Newswire (CN)**
Christian Communication Network's Christian Newswire will send press releases to your specified target audience for a fee. Publishers and authors can choose from a list of 1,200 Christian radio, television, and print outlets nationwide or over 350 Catholic media outlets.
www.earnedmedia.org

- **CLASS Promotional Services, LLC**
This organization offers a publicity service for Christian authors. For a fee, CLASS Promotional Services will book interviews on Christian radio and/or Christian television for Christian authors seeking to promote their books.
www.classervices.com

The following services are geared toward general market radio and television media outlets.

- *Radio and TV Interview Report*

    This magazine is produced three times each month and sent to over 4,000 radio and television producers across the United States and Canada.
    www.rtir.com

- GuestFinder

    This online listing service is designed to make it easy for people who work in the media to find guest and interview sources. It also provides an inexpensive way for talented professionals to announce their availability as media guests.
    www.guestfinder.com

- PR Web

    Press Release Newswire offers free online press release distribution services. They are the largest newswire catering to small- and medium-sized companies and one of the largest online press release newswires. PR Web is a general market press release service.
    www.prweb.com

2. Local Radio Stations

If you are new to public speaking and radio interviews you can start with local Christian radio shows to acquire practice and experience with interviewing prior to taking on a national radio or television campaign. Interviews on local Christian radio stations can provide good publicity for your book. Local radio stations will be more likely to list you on their websites, announce your website and ordering information more frequently during an interview, and even ask you back for subsequent interviews, than the larger national radio shows and stations.

When seeking to secure an interview on a local radio station, make sure that your pitch letter includes the title of your book, your credentials, how your topic addresses current events, and why it is right for the show's audience. Include an accompanying list of 10 to 15 potential interview questions for the producer and copies of relevant reviews, endorsements, and newspaper articles you have secured on your book. Some authors send a copy of their book with their pitch letter. However, don't just rely on your press releases and pitch letters to obtain interviews. Radio personnel are generally more auditory than visual. You will need to phone station producers after sending your queries to verbally request a guest interview. Producers need to feel secure that you will be entertaining and interesting enough to hold their audience's attention. Sometimes repeat phone calls are required to secure an interview.

Local Christian radio stations can easily be located by using a radio station finder on the Internet.

- Radio-Locator

    This comprehensive Internet radio station search engine features links to over 10,000 radio station web pages. Searches can be made by city or state as well as for radio station format such as religious, Christian contemporary, or gospel music.
    www.radio-locator.com

- ChristianRadio.com

    This website features 2,500 Christian radio stations searchable by state. The site also includes links to Christian radio networks that broadcast programming through many Christian radio stations.
    www.christianradio.com

- **Catholic Radio Association**
  This association's website allows browsers to search for member Catholic radio stations by state.
  www.catholicradioassociation.org

Christian Mail-Order Catalogs

A listing in a mail-order catalog can place your book in front of thousands of Christian consumers. There are mail-order catalogs for literally every interest. Many Christian-themed mail-order catalogs primarily feature gift items with only a few books. These companies look for books that make good "gift" books.

The Directory of Mail-Order Catalogs is a good resource for finding catalogs to approach with your book. This directory lists over 10,000 catalogs that are offered in print. The following are two Christian catalogs that are a good starting place for those seeking to secure space in mail-order catalogs.

- **Christian Book Distributors (CBD)**
  CBD is the world's largest mail-order catalog company.

  Christian Book Distributors
  P.O. Box 6000
  Peabody, MA 01961
  800-247-4784
  www.christianbooks.com

- **Christian Tools of Affirmation (CTA)**
  CTA provides purposeful products to help encourage God's people. The catalog features mostly gift products, but books that make good gifts are also included.

CTA, Inc.
1625 Larkin Williams Rd.
P.O. Box 1205
Fenton, MO 63026
www.ctainc.com

Another consideration closely tied to mail-order catalogs is home show businesses. These businesses are run with a tiered structure where consultants sell products through home-based show parties. These businesses generally require a fairly steep discount (up to 80%) on products as they must sell a product for four to five times its cost to them to make a profit. You may find a niche for your books in either a Christian-themed home show business or a general home show business that carries some religious products. One example of a Christian-themed home show business is:

- **Good Books & Company**

    This home show company offers carefully selected products including books about living the Christian life, Bible studies, fiction, children's books, and gift items all related to faith and friendship.

    Good Books & Company
    7814 Potomac Dr.
    Colorado Springs, CO 80920
    www.goodbooksandcompany.com

Christian Organizations

Christian organizations and associations exist for every group of people: mothers, fathers, women, men, military, disabled, farmers, and nurses; to name just a few. Whatever the target market is for your book, a Christian organization already exists that provides services to this demographic.

Many opportunities exist for marketing your books through these Christian organizations. Most of these organizations hold national or regional conferences where publishers can exhibit books or advertise in conference publications. All provide some type of written publication to their members or target group that publishes articles and displays ads.

Some provide their members an online store or catalog from which to purchase materials that speak to their unique situation. You can find economical ways to market through these organizations to reach large numbers of your target audience.

The number of Christian organizations that exist is astounding. Christian organizations and associations can be actual physical entities or they may be just web-based ministries ministering only through the online media. Below is a listing of a few of the larger Christian organizations that are both a physical entity and hold a web presence.

- **Catholic Association of Musicians (CAM)**
    CAM provides support to both the liturgical and non-liturgical Catholic musicians that work in service to the Catholic Church.
    www.cammusic.com

- **Christian Military Fellowship (CMF)**
    CMF supports United States military personnel and their families worldwide with local fellowships, conferences, and Christian resources.
    www.cmfhq.org

- **Focus on the Family**

    This ministry, led by Dr. James Dobson, ministers to today's Christian family through a large number of different programs.

    www.family.org

- **Joni and Friends**

    This organization, led by Joni Eareckson Tada, communicates the gospel and equips churches worldwide to minister to people affected by disability.

    www.joniandfriends.org

- **MOPS™**

    MOPS stands for Mothers of Preschoolers and ministers to mothers of preschool-aged children in small groups around the country.

    www.mops.org

- **Prison Fellowship®**

    Founded by Chuck Colson, Prison Fellowship partners with local churches across the country to minister to prisoners, ex-prisoners, and their families.

    www.pfm.org

- **Promise Keepers®**

    Promise Keepers is a ministry for men. This group strives to ignite and unite men to be passionate followers of Jesus Christ through adhering to seven basic principles. They hold regional conferences around the country.

    www.promisekeepers.org

- **Proverbs 31 Ministries™**
    This organization endeavors to bring God's peace, perspective, and purpose to today's busy women.
    www.proverbs31.org

A few lists of Christian ministries can be found on the web. Gospelcom.net Alliance hosts over 230 different Christian ministries that range greatly in size, vision, and purpose. You can find Gospelcom.net Alliance's list of ministries at www.gospelcom.net/ministries. Two more online lists of Christian ministries can be found at www.centralpc.org/links/links1.htm#orgs and www.iclnet.org/pub/resources/xn-dir2.html.

Christian Schools

Christian schools purchase books to supplement their curriculum. Schools need good reading material for their libraries and classrooms. Publishers with books aimed at children, teenagers, or Christian school teachers can tap this market to access more Christian consumers. There are Christian schools in every community across the United States representing hundreds of thousands of reading children, their families, and their teachers.

1. Christian School Associations
The most effective way to reach this market is through established Christian school associations that Christian schools affiliate with. Most Christian school associations represent schools that include programs for preschool through high school. These associations feature national and regional teacher conferences where publishers can exhibit materials and advertise in conference publications. Many also have newsletters or journals that are sent to

member schools on a regular basis providing you yet another avenue to place your books in front of this audience. Mailing list rentals of member schools are also available from many of the Christian school associations.

The larger Christian school associations are listed here.

- **American Association of Christian Schools (AACS)**
    AACS is one of the leading Christian school associations in the United States with over 1,000 member schools.
    www.aacs.org

- **Association of Christian Schools International (ACSI)**
    ACSI is one of the largest Christian school associations with eighteen regional offices around the world.
    www.acsi.org

- **Association of Christian Teachers and Schools (ACTS)**
    ACTS is an association for Assembly of God schools and teachers across the country.
    www.acts.ag.org

- **Association of Classical and Christian Schools (ACCS)**
    ACCS is an association of Christian schools dedicated to teaching a classical approach to education.
    www.accsedu.org

- **Evangelical Lutheran Education Association (ELEA)**
    ELEA is an association for Evangelical Lutheran schools and early childhood programs (preschools).
    www.eleanational.org

- **National Catholic Education Association (NCEA)**
    NCEA is an association of Catholic parochial schools.
    www.ncea.org

- **Southern Baptist Association of Christian Schools (SBACS)**
    The Southern Baptist Church is one of the largest church denominations in the United States and SBACS has a sizeable number of member schools.
    www.sbacs.org

2. Book Fairs

Many Christian schools also hold book fairs where students, teachers, and parents can purchase books. These book fairs help raise money for the school as well as provide the students and their families with quality reading material. You can submit your books for consideration to companies that provide book fair services to Christian schools. Many of the book fair companies provide a range of books from many publishers. Two companies providing book fair services to Christian schools are listed here.

- **Concordia Christian Book Fair**
    This program is run by Concordia Publishing House. The book fair carries books from multiple publishers as well as Concordia's own books.
    www.bookfairs.cph.org

- **God's World Book Club**
    This book club is a program of God's World Publications which publishes *World Magazine* along with other magazines. They provide book fairs to Christian schools as well as a catalog.
    www.gwbc.com

3. Mailing Lists

Mailing list rental companies also rent lists of Christian and parochial school addresses. For example, American Church Lists' complete list of Christian and parochial schools contains over 15,000 elementary schools, 12,000 middle schools, and 6,400 high schools. You can find American Church Lists online at www.americanchurchlists.com.

4. Christian Colleges and Seminaries

In considering Christian schools, don't overlook Christian colleges, Bible schools, and seminaries if this market is appropriate for your books. One reasonably good (although not comprehensive) list of these types of schools can be found on the web at www.csrnet.org/csrnet/colleges.html. Another resource is the Council for Christian Colleges and Universities (CCCU), which provides a variety of services to its 105 member schools in North America. You can find CCCU online at www.cccu.org. For more on marketing to Bible schools and seminaries see Chapter 7, Connect with Churches.

Christian Camps and Conference Centers

Thousands of Christian camps and conference centers cater to millions of families and children each year. Most of these camps and centers include a gift shop where attendees can purchase gifts, books, and other material. These camp and conference center gift shops provide another avenue for you to make your books available to more Christian consumers.

The majority of camp and conference center gift store managers (most of whom are the camp director or one of the staff) do not attend Christian retail tradeshows, nor are these stores CBA members. Camp and conference center gift stores tend to be small stores (much like many churches are now beginning to host small bookstores in their facilities for their attendees) with very limited shelf space. Sales representatives, product catalogs, and word-of-mouth are how most of these stores decide on which products to stock.

If you have a book that would do well in this market, consider attempting to tap the Christian camp and conference center marketplace. Since most Christian camps and conference centers strive to promote spiritual growth for their attendees, books that fall into this category lend themselves to this market. Other books that also do well in this environment are books for children and teenagers, books on family matters, and gift books.

Most Christian camps and conference centers belong to a camp and conference center association. These associations rent their mailing lists, provide some type of publication to their members (magazine, newsletter, or e-zine) that you can advertise in, and host annual conferences where you can exhibit your titles.

Following are some Christian camp and conference center associations to consider.

- **Christian Camp and Conference Association (CCCA)**

    This large association provides extensive programs, products, and services to autonomous Christian camps and conference centers nationwide. Their website contains the most extensive online database of Christian camps, conference centers, and retreat centers.
    http://cci.gospelcom.net/ccihome

- **Southern Baptist Camping Association**
  The Southern Baptist Church has numerous Christian camps across the country that are affiliated with their denomination.
  www.sbcamping.org

- **Mennonite Camping Association**
  This association is for camps belonging to Mennonite congregations and holding to those tenets of belief.
  www.mennonitecamping.org

- **National Association of Christian Camps (NACC)**
  This organization has about 30 member camps and lists an additional 40 Christian camps across the United States on their website.
  www.naccamps.org

- **Young Life Camping**
  Young Life, an organization for middle and high school students, owns 23 camps across the country.
  www.younglife.org/Camping/ylcamping.html

An additional resource for religious camp listings online is www.mysummercamps.com. Mysummercamps.com hosts the web's most comprehensive list of camps. You can search for camps by religious affiliation (i.e., Anglican, Catholic, Methodist, or Presbyterian). This is a great resource for finding camps of various denominations that may not have their own camping association.

Author Book Signings

Authors who are willing to do book signings bring publishers an effective low-cost marketing tool. As an author, you do not need to be a known personality to have a successful book signing, nor do you need to embark on a national book signing tour to be effective. Start with where you live and schedule book signings at local Christian and general market bookstores in your town and surrounding communities. CBA (Christian Booksellers Association) encourages their member stores to host Christian author book signings as a way to increase store traffic. When scheduling book signings don't overlook local Barnes & Noble Booksellers and Borders® stores. Both of these bookstore chains are open to selling local authors' books as well as scheduling local author talks and book signings.

Once you have scheduled a book signing, don't expect the bookstore to handle all the promotion of the event. Publishers should provide the bookstore with posters announcing the book, author, and book signing date. Press releases should be sent to all local media regarding the upcoming book signing including the store location, date, and time of the event. If the Christian bookstore hosting the book signing has a list of local church congregations, use this list to send announcements (via snail mail or email) to local churches to include in their Sunday bulletins or on a community notice bulletin board. Publishers should list authors' appearances on their websites and authors should also list appearances on their individual websites. It is important to have plenty of promotional materials for book signings. Bookmarks, postcards, and even pens or pencils can all help promote the book during and after the signing event.

Forming alliances with other authors provides ways to expose more Christian consumers to your books. Readers of another author's books may begin to read your books if that author recommends your titles through cross-promotion. Alliances offer you opportunities for joint book signings. Hosting a multiple author book signing, especially for new authors, can be a useful tool. A book signing featuring two, three, or four local authors draws more attention and brings in more Christian consumers. Alliances also provide other ways for you to cross-promote each others' books including website links and selling each others' titles at signings.

You can also form alliances with Christian music groups. More and more Christian authors are teaming with Christian artists as they tour. In this type of alliance, the author usually speaks to the audience for a short part of the musicians' concert. This type of partnership allows Christian artists and authors to cross-promote each others' works.

Consider holding a contest during your book signing offering a free prize to the winner. The prize offered for such a contest is best if it is something other than a book. Offering something related to the book's topic or theme works best. For example, if you have a cookbook or health book with recipes, you could offer an apron or special mixing bowl set. A contest does not need to be elaborate. You can simply have consumers leave a business card or paper with contact information in a bowl and let them know that the winner will be notified by telephone and will be able to pick up the prize at the bookstore following the book signing event.

Creativity can pay off at book signing events and draw attention from customers who may not normally stop. One example of this would be that for a book on Christianity and martial arts, the author could wear a martial arts uniform to the book signing. Or, for a book on the Fruit of the Spirit, place a large fruit display on or near the author's signing table to draw customers' attention.

When the book signing is finished, arrange to sign a few copies of the featured book for the bookstore and provide "Autographed by Author" stickers for these books. Also remember to follow up with a thank you note to the bookstore for hosting the book signing event.

To find CBA member Christian bookstores in a given area, simply visit http://cba.know-where.com/cba.

Author Speaking Engagements

Christian authors willing to travel, speak, and sign books gain more attention from Christian consumers for their books. Some authors have single-handedly propelled their books to bestseller status by their willingness to travel, speak, and sign books on a continual basis. If you, like many authors, do not have the ability to travel and speak extensively due to other life commitments, don't overlook this important aspect of book marketing. Authors who are willing to do even a few speaking engagements will develop a loyal reader base and increase book sales.

All sorts of Christian events feature authors as speakers. Christian speakers are needed for events ranging from local women's conferences to church youth retreats to national conferences for Christians. There are a number of Christian directories that help Christian leaders find Christian speakers for their upcoming events.

- **Christian Speaker Net**

    Christian Speaker Net is an online listing of affordable Christian speakers. The site is quite cost effective for Christian speakers to list their profile and contact information. Christian churches and organizations seeking speakers for events can search this directory to find a Christian speaker.
    www.christianspeaker.net

- **CLASServices, Inc.**

  CLASS offers seminars and conferences each year to train individuals as Christian speakers. To be listed as a speaker with CLASS, an individual must complete their training program and meet other qualifications listed on their website.

  www.classervices.com

- **AWSA**

  Advanced Writers and Speakers Association is an organization for Christian women who have written at least two books and speak to groups of 100 people at least three times per year.

  www.awsawomen.com

- **Good Girl Book Club™**

  Good Girl Book Club is an online literary ministry for young and adult Christian women. Membership in the club is free and Good Girl Book Club reports to reach over 125,000 Christian women worldwide. The ministry includes Christian Author Network™. Listing in this network is reasonably priced and includes a personal page. Christian organizations seeking authors for book signings or speaking engagements can search this directory.

  www.goodgirlbookclubonline.com

Public Libraries

While public libraries are not Christian institutions, large numbers of Christians frequent public libraries and borrow books. As a result, many libraries feature Christian titles for their patrons. Public libraries across the country purchase large numbers of books.

Placing your title in front of public library book buyers can result in book sales.

For libraries to purchase them, your books should contain a Library of Congress Control Number (LCCN) and should be listed with a library jobber (a wholesaler that librarians purchase from). Three major library jobbers are Baker & Taylor at **www.btol.com**, Brodart at **www.books.brodart.com**, and Midwest Library Services at **www.midwestls.com**. Brodart allows publishers to list titles in their database for free. They then order your title when a librarian places an order with them for that title.

There are a number of good ways to market your books to public libraries.

- **Advertisements in Library Journals**

The foremost publications libraries use to determine what books to buy are *Booklist*, *Library Journal*, *Publishers Weekly*, and *ForeWord Magazine*. Besides striving to have your book reviewed in one of these publications, which will virtually guarantee sales of your book to libraries, you can place advertisements in these periodicals as another venue for bringing your titles before library book buyers.

- **Direct Mail**

You can rent a public library mailing list such as one that is offered at **www.mailings.com** and send your brochure or catalog directly to libraries. Another option is to participate in cooperative mailing programs to libraries such as the one that PMA (**www.pmaonline.org**) provides for its member publishers.

- **Library Association Meetings**

The most cost-effective way to exhibit your titles at national and state library association meetings is to use an exhibit service such as

Combined Book Exhibit at www.combinedbook.com. This service provides book presentation at the major library association meetings for a reasonable fee.

- **Friends of the Library Groups**

Friends of the Library groups exist to support local public libraries. Most public libraries have such a group. These groups raise financial and community support for a library. Many of these groups publish newsletters that are made available to library patrons, and they schedule author speaking engagements for their local library. As an author, you can submit articles for these newsletters and alert your local public libraries' Friends of the Library groups of your willingness to be a featured speaker at a library.

To submit information to any particular Friends of the Library group, simply mail your correspondence to:

>Friends of the Library
>c/o Library Name
>Library Address

A comprehensive list of public libraries listed by state can be found on the web at http://lists.webjunction.org/libweb/Public_main.html.

Creative Marketing

1. Contests

Creative thinking leads to great promotional ideas. One Christian publisher recently sponsored a contest on one of their fiction author's books. They invited fans to publicize the author's new book and submit the results of their publicity efforts via email to the publisher. The winner received an expense paid trip to a women's conference to hear the author speak and had a character named after her in the author's next book. Another author featured a riddle in her book and offered a cash prize to the first five readers who solved the riddle.

2. Partner with a Charity

Another creative idea is to partner with a Christian non-profit charity or service organization to develop a bookmark, magnet, or other promotional item featuring a principal statement or quote from one of your books. This magnet or bookmark would also include the title of the book, the publisher's contact information, and the name and contact information of the charity organization. The non-profit organization would include this promotional item in its direct mail solicitations for donations as a free gift to potential donors. You would pay for the cost of the promotional item while the charity group would pay the mailing costs.

This type of promotion benefits both you and the charity organization as it allows both your book and the organization's name to be advertised. The amount of exposure received for your book would be as great as the size of the non-profit organization's mailing list.

Harness the Internet 9

*The race is not to the swift or the battle to the strong,
nor does food come to the wise or wealth to the brilliant
or favor to the learned; but time and chance happen to them all.*
—*Ecclesiastes 9:11*

THE INTERNET HAS BECOME an integral part of life for Americans. Nearly 75% of adults in the United States have Internet access and at least 25% of these adults use the Internet to get religious information and connect with others about faith. Over 10% of all books are bought online.

In 2002, books were the most prolific product sold on the Internet with 43% of online shoppers purchasing at least one book. As the Internet continues to become entrenched in people's everyday lives, book buying online will also continue to escalate. In today's market, the Internet cannot be ignored. Publishers and authors must learn to harness the Internet to promote and sell books.

Websites

Every publisher should have a website. Publishers should also sponsor websites for each of their authors. A web presence is an essential element of a marketing plan for books.

However, with growing e-commerce, merely having a website is not enough. As Internet use continues to grow, your business website must not only attract visitors, it must also be "convincing" so that visitors who find your website will actually purchase your products. Having convincing website material can make all the difference in converting website visitors to buyers. Convincing website material includes:

1. Testimonials

Your website should provide testimonials from satisfied customers and reviews from known industry book reviewers. Testimonials increase your website visitors' confidence that a book is worth the money they will invest in purchasing it. However, be sure to obtain permission from your sources prior to posting their names and quotes on your website.

2. Associations, Affiliations, and Awards

Membership in a recognized industry association, along with the appearance of that association's logo on your website, can be convincing to visitors because it adds legitimacy and validates your business. Posting awards that you have received for your books increases the odds that visitors will purchase a book.

3. Offering a Freebie

Freebies can take a number of forms and serve the purpose of inviting visitors to connect with your material. A sneak preview of a book through posting a chapter or two from that book is one type of freebie. This type of freebie is comparable to Amazon.com's® "Search Inside™" program which was developed to encourage customers to purchase books. Another type of freebie is a website posting of an article on a related topic to a book's theme made available for a visitor to read or download. Freebies can also be a product that you throw in for free when a customer purchases your book. Your free product can be as small as a bookmark or as large as an additional book (maybe a title you are phasing out and want to clear out of your backstock).

4. Contact Information

Many small business web pages lack specific contact information other than an email address. Placing specific contact information (address and phone number) increases visitors' security that your business is "real." It also increases visitors' confidence that if they encounter a problem in ordering they will be able to speak with a person about the problem.

Once you have developed a "convincing" website, your next challenge is to draw visitors to your website to view your material. There are a number of avenues available online to help draw traffic to your website as well as to market your books to potential purchasers.

Affiliate Programs

Affiliate programs are a referral-based marketing strategy designed to increase your online sales. This type of program allows you (the publisher) to post advertisements on other businesses' websites (the affiliates). You (the publisher) only pay the other websites (affiliates) for your posted advertisements when customers connect to your website through the advertisements and make a purchase. You pay a commission (generally a percentage of the sale) to the website owner whose advertisement brought the customer to your online store.

The way this basically works is a website (affiliate) agrees to post a banner link showing your (the publisher's) products. When the affiliate website's visitors click on the banner, these visitors are linked to your website. If the visitor makes a purchase from your website, you then pay the affiliate (website posting the banner link) a commission for each book sold from the banner link click-through.

Affiliate programs account for about 20% of the $53 billion in revenue currently generated online. Marketing through affiliate programs is a great low-cost way to advertise. You do not pay for banner placement or advertising, you only pay for results. If an affiliate drives visitors to your site, but these visitors don't purchase, you don't owe the affiliate any money.

The largest affiliate program on the web is Amazon.com. Starting in 1996, the Amazon Associates program was the first online affiliate program of its kind. Today, it is the largest and most successful online affiliate program, with over 900,000 members joining worldwide. Website owners earn from 4% up to 10.5% in referral fees when a customer purchases products on Amazon.com from using a "Buy Amazon" banner link on their website.

If you choose not to have a shopping cart for visitors to purchase books directly from your website, you can sign up to become an Amazon Associate. Amazon.com will provide you a "Buy Amazon" link which you then place on your webpage allowing your website visitors to purchase your books through Amazon.com. In return, Amazon will pay you a referral fee for each book purchased.

To register your website as an Associate with Amazon.com visit www.amazon.com and click on the "Associates" button.

If you are selling your books directly from your website and wish to develop your own affiliate program to increase website traffic and book sales, it is possible to develop an effective affiliate program. The cost to you is the time it takes to find and recruit websites whose visitors would most likely be interested in your books. For example, if you sell Bible-study materials, you could search for those websites that cater to individuals interested in learning more about the Bible and approach these websites to encourage them to become an affiliate for your products.

When establishing your own affiliate program, tracking technology is required to effectively track which sites your sales come from. You can establish your own affiliate program, purchase tracking software, and pay commissions directly to your affiliates; or you can use an existing affiliate service that tracks the commissions for you. Two such affiliate services are www.clickbank.com and www.refer-it.com.

Affiliate programs offer a great online marketing tool that is very cost-effective since payment is only made when a sale occurs. This type of marketing increases both traffic to your website and sales of your books.

e-Newsletters

e-Newsletters (also called e-zines) are another low-cost Internet marketing tool. The goal of e-newsletters is to turn visitors into customers and to create a base of clients loyal to your books. Two main avenues exist to promote books through e-newsletters.

1. Create Your Own

Publishers and authors can use an e-newsletter to connect with readers and website visitors to develop a loyal customer base for your books. Publishers utilizing e-newsletters to reach consumers should include articles from their authors in their e-newsletters and encourage their authors to have a link to sign up for the publisher's e-newsletter on their individual author websites. e-Newsletter material should include supplementary information on subjects from existing books as well as excerpts from upcoming books to encourage readers to purchase.

The challenge in creating and launching an e-newsletter is acquiring subscribers. To begin, you can utilize contact information from individuals who have purchased your books and include a way for website visitors to sign up for your free e-newsletter on your website. Once a base of readers is established, managing the email list for your newsletter is the next challenge. Software is available for managing email mailing lists. An example of email list software can be found at **www.rkssoftware.com**. Online services that help with managing email lists are also available. Some of these mailing list services are free such as http://freegroups.net and some charge a monthly fee that varies based on the size of your email list such as www.constantcontact.com and www.intellicontact.com.

2. Advertise in an Existing e-Newsletter

Some e-newsletters call advertising "advertisements" while others call it "sponsorships." Either way, it is paying an existing e-newsletter for an advertisement to promote your books to a large audience. Since there is no central registry or search engine for e-newsletters, if you choose to advertise in e-newsletters, you must research to find ones that fit your target audience.

There are a few e-zine directories online that provide lists of e-newsletters by subject such as www.ezinelisting.com, www.ezine-dir.com, and www.ezinelocater.com. However, these directories are limited in their listings of Christian-based e-zines.

A few Christian sites provide listings of faith-based e-newsletters. These include www.christianitytoday.com/free/features/newsletters.html, which lists all the e-newsletters produced by Christianity Today International, and www.gospelcom.net/ministries/newsletters, which features a listing of Gospelcom.net ministries' e-newsletters.

Another option for advertising in e-newsletters that does not require as much research is to place advertisements through free mailing list services online. Many free mailing list services pay for their list management through tacking advertisements onto the emails sent through their service. You can place advertisements with these services and reach a large group of consumers without having to find specific e-newsletters to advertise with.

An example of this is Christian eMail Service. Geared toward the Christian community (list owners are mostly churches and Christian businesses), Christian eMail Service offers their list management services for free. Placing an ad with Christian eMail Service allows you to advertise to a wide cross-section of Christian consumers. This service can be found at www.christianemailservice.com.

Email Campaigns

An email marketing campaign is similar to a direct snail-mail campaign except that the marketing is done via email addresses over the Internet rather than physical addresses through the post office. Email campaigns are more cost effective than direct mail campaigns. Email campaigns increase their effectiveness when repeat messages are used (email messages are sent repeatedly over a period of time).

Research indicates that Friday is the best day of the work week to conduct an email marketing campaign. While more than a third of email messages are opened on any given day, Friday consistently outperforms the other days for the percent of messages read.

Many of the companies that provide postal list rentals for targeted audiences also provide email list rentals. There are also Internet companies that specialize in providing targeted email marketing services. Three such companies are Church World Direct at www.cwd.com, ExactTarget at www.exacttarget.com and Catholic Online at www.catholic.org.

Blogs

A blog (a short term for web log) is a personal journal of thoughts and ideas posted on the World Wide Web. These personal journals are generally updated daily or weekly with the blog author's opinions and musings. Blogs are currently one of the fastest-growing phenomena on the Internet. There are a number of ways that publishers and authors can use blogs to generate traffic to their website and to increase the exposure of their books to Christian consumers.

1. Create a Blog

Creating a blog can generate traffic to your website and increase your books' sales, even with the thousands of blogs currently published on the web. When blogs were first created in 1994 (long before the term "blog" was used) so few existed that each web log had no problem hooking plenty of readers. Today, with automated publishing systems for blogs, there is now a plethora of blogs (you can literally find a blog on any subject) and thus hooking regular readers takes more effort.

The greatest challenge with a blog (as with a website) is generating a following of people who read your blog regularly. Authors and publishers who already publish an e-newsletter have a ready made audience from which to generate regular blog readers. These readers will in turn increase your blog traffic through word-of-mouth to other potential readers. However, even if you do not have a ready-made audience to read your blog, starting a blog can still increase your website traffic and your books' exposure.

There are many tools on the web that allow you to create and maintain a blog for free. However, blogs do take time. They are a personal journal and need to be updated regularly. Additionally, blog thoughts and musing should tie in to the subjects of your books. You need to have a variety of thoughts on these subjects which you can write about on a regular basis.

Publishers can encourage their authors to create blogs. Established authors have a ready made audience to draw from. Consumers who have read and appreciated an author's book are likely to follow a blog posted by that author, especially if the blog continues the themes started in the author's book(s) and provides sneak peaks at upcoming projects. Publishers creating a blog can encourage their authors to post on their blog and include links to their authors' blogs to generate interest in their authors' books.

Blogs can be posted and maintained on your existing website or maintained separately through one of the many free blog spots on the web. Authors and publishers who choose to blog on their existing website have the additional work of submitting their blog to blog indexes and search engines on the web to generate traffic. There are a number of search engines dedicated to finding blogs such as www.globeofblogs.com. Both Google™ and Yahoo™ also have search engines designed to find blogs.

A number of blog sites online provide free blog space to users. These sites provide easy user-friendly tools for publishing and keeping a blog updated. They also have automatic RSS feeds that alert readers when a site's content is updated. Utilizing a free blog site can generate immediate additional traffic for your blog (and subsequently your website) as these blog sites already have existing customers providing you potential walk-through traffic. Free online blog sites include www.blogger.com, www.faces.com, and www.blog-city.com.

Even better than a general free blog site is a free blog site that is specific to your subject matter. Subject-specific blog sites provide a blogger with many potential readers from a pool of individuals who are already interested in your subject. This type of blog site allows you to maximize your blogging. Two examples of free subject-specific blog sites are www.homeschoolblogger.com, a blog site geared toward homeschoolers, and www.travelpod.com, for those blogs pertaining to travel.

The challenge with a blog (as with any website) lies not in creating and maintaining the blog, but in acquiring traffic—getting people to visit and read your blog. If your existing website already generates a substantial amount of traffic, then adding a blog on your website can serve to increase repeat customers as well as generate additional traffic. If your website could use a boost in traffic, then creating a blog with a free blog service can potentially bring new traffic to your existing website and widen the audience for your books.

2. Advertise on Existing Blogs

While blogs are still by and large personal web logs, they are rapidly becoming a form of public relations for businesses. As a result, many blogs are now posting advertisements just like websites.

Posting advertisements on those blogs related to your books' topics is a great marketing strategy.

For finding blogs on which to post advertisements, a couple of options are available. You can conduct your own blog search using lists of Christian blog aggregators and sites such as the listings on www.smartchristian.com or www.blogs4god.com and then approach each viable blog site individually with your request to advertise. The other option is to use an existing blog ad service such as www.blogads.com where blogs are broken down by category (e.g., evangelical, homeschooling, and parenting) with a listing of blogs that are currently accepting ads. This service has you indicate which blogs you want to advertise on and they facilitate the deal.

3. Get Your Books Reviewed on Blogs

Many bloggers post book reviews on their blog sites. There are a number of Christian bloggers who are reviewing books and posting book reviews. With most bloggers, a book need not be pre-publication or brand new for the blogger to consider a review. Some bloggers will review books that have been available for awhile if the topic of the book fits with their blog subject and will generate interest from their blog readers.

Again, as with blog advertisements, you can choose to find blogs to review your books or you can utilize a blog book review service. There are a few bloggers focused on providing their readers reviews of books. Examples of these include http://catholicbooks.blogspot.com, providing reviews of Catholic books, www.suburbansista.blogspot.com, for African-American books, and www.ebookreader.blogspot.com, for small press e-books.

To find individual bloggers willing to review your books, you can utilize a blog search engine to search for blogs by subject. Online blog search engines include www.blogsearch.google.com, www.blogsearchengine.com, and www.blogdigger.com. When you have identified potential blogs, you can then approach these individual bloggers with a request to review your book.

Searching out bloggers who provide book reviews can be time consuming, so for those publishers who desire to have an efficient means of getting your books in the hands of bloggers who post reviews, a blog book review service is your answer. Active Christian Media hosts a blog review service that caters to the Christian and conservative crowds. For a fee, Active Christian Media will distribute your book to Christian or conservative bloggers for review on their blogs. This service can be found online at **www.blogforbooks.com**.

WebRings

A WebRing is a network of related websites. Websites with similar content are grouped together in a "ring" with each site linked to another in the group by a navigation bar (link box) on each of the group members' websites. A WebRing is created and maintained by an individual website owner called the RingMaster who ensures that the websites in the Ring all fit the Ring topic.

Joining a WebRing can bring new traffic to your website. Visitors to other sites in the WebRing interested in more sites on that selected topic can use the navigation bar to visit the other websites of the Ring (including your website). Best of all, WebRings are a free tool for increasing website traffic as there is no cost to join.

To increase traffic to your website, you can create your own WebRing and invite other websites to join, or you can join an existing WebRing. The WebRing service can be found online at **www.webring.com**. WebRing hosts over 1,000 Christian-themed WebRings on the Internet including WebRings for Christian author websites.

To find, join, or create your own Ring, just follow the instructions and links on the website at www.webring.com. Joining and creating WebRings is free. However, this service also provides fee-based opportunities for additional website promotion and advertisements. These include having your website featured prominently on the WebRing and placements of targeted banner ads.

Online Communities

Online communities exist for every target audience you can think of. These communities host chat rooms, discussion forums, discussion groups, articles, and helpful links; they publish e-newsletters and feature advertisements. They present many opportunities for publishers and authors to promote books. Most online communities are free to join.

Authors can join online communities that match their books' subjects and find opportunities to promote their books through article submissions and discussion boards. Publishers can find many advertising opportunities through online communities.

There are too many online communities to list here. Below is just a sampling of the online communities geared toward Christian moms.

- www.christianmom.com
- www.momsoffaith.com
- www.gentlechristianmothers.com
- www.christian-mommies.com
- www.seriousmoms.com
- www.christianmomstalk.com
- www.christianwomensresources.com

Online Bookstores

In marketing books, the more avenues through which your books are available for readers to purchase, the more books you will be able to sell. Ease of ordering and purchasing is important for today's consumers. There are literally thousands of online bookstores on the Internet. Your books do not need to be listed with every bookstore, but listing with the main online bookstores is extremely important. Fortunately, listing with the main online bookstores is relatively easy as these bookstores strive to make every possible in-print book available to customers.

- **Amazon.com®**

    Amazon.com has a program for small publishers called Amazon Advantage. For a small yearly fee, they list and sell your books on their site and pay you 45% of the sale. To access the information for this program, click on the Advantage hotlink on their home page. If your titles are listed in a major distributor's catalog (such as Ingram/Spring Arbor or Baker & Taylor) your titles automatically appear on Amazon.com. Amazon.com then places orders for books (as they sell) through the distributor in whose catalog your titles appear.
    www.amazon.com

- **Barnes&Noble.com**

    Barnes&Noble.com will list almost any book on their website if their submission guidelines are followed. To find the submission guidelines for Barnes&Noble.com visit their home page and click on the "Publishers and Authors Guidelines" link on the bottom of that page.
    www.bn.com

- **Christianbook.com**

    This online bookstore is owned by Christian Book Distributors (CBD). It is the largest Christian bookstore on the Internet. Christianbook.com will list any Christian title that is available through Spring Arbor. Contact information is available on their website.
    www.christianbook.com

Another large online bookstore worth mentioning is eBay at www.ebay.com. While eBay functions as an online auction house for any item, many companies and individuals sell books on eBay through both their auction process and their "Buy It Now" program. You can sign up to be a seller on eBay and offer books for sale through this avenue in addition to the other major online bookstores.

Creative Marketing

1. A-Page-A-Day

One self-publisher developed a novel approach to selling books over the Internet. His concept is "give your book away for profit." To help consumers reach the purchase point, he emails one page of his book each day to those individuals who sign up to receive the free "A-Page-A-Day" on his website. These page-a-day emails are sent automatically using autoresponders. You can learn more about A-Page-A-Day and the steps to create your own book giveaway at www.bookresponder.com.

2. Book Previews

As technology advances, so must the marketing tools for gaining consumers interest in books. Some small Christian publishing houses have embraced a new marketing technology and have begun to utilize Book Trailers™ in their book marketing efforts. Book Trailers are just what they sound like; a movie trailer-like presentation for a book. Combining dramatic scenes, music, and narration, these creative mini-films allow customers to catch a glimpse into a book. They remind the viewer that books are movies of the mind. Played in movie theaters prior to the feature presentation, as advertisements on cable television and on websites over the internet; book previews are catching on and publishers are beginning to embrace this new creative book promotion technique.

Circle of Seven Productions (www.cosproductions.com) is one of the pioneers in this new marketing technique. They created and trademarked the terms Book Trailer™ (for movie theaters) and Book Teaser™ (for television). While they are not the only production company producing book preview videos, they are the only ones using the terms Book Trailer or Book Teaser.

Other producers have jumped on board with the book preview concept. Book Stream, Inc. (www.bookstreaminc.com), has developed BookWraps™ which is a combination of author interview with author video combined with text information about the book. Expanded Books™ (www.expandedbooks.com) produces videos where the author is interviewed and has dramatic scenes play as the author talks. Vidlit™ (www.vidlit.com) uses comic-book type graphics with author narration for their videos.

This innovative book marketing technique is worth considering. It appeals to the current multi-media population and it harnesses the Internet in an unprecedented way for book promotion.

Summary

An Internet presence has become an essential ingredient in success for book producers. The Internet is vast and the opportunities it holds for promotion are endless. Creative use of the Internet can lead to great promotional ideas that, in today's day and age, spread rapidly among Internet users. Whole books are dedicated to this subject. While this chapter has barely scratched the surface of harnessing the Internet to promote your books, hopefully it has at least served to get you started on the path to promoting your Christian books on the Internet.

Handle Overstocks and Remainders 10

In his heart a man plans his course, but the Lord determines his steps.
—Proverbs 16:9

SOMETIMES DESPITE YOUR BEST EFFORTS, a title may not sell as well as you anticipated. So what is a publisher to do with too much inventory? Too much inventory can come in the form of remainders (books left over when you have discontinued a title) or overstocks (needing to make room for new titles). Sooner or later most publishers face this dilemma either from printing too many copies of a book that does not sell as well as expected or when discontinuing a title that has run its course. One option is to sell these books to a bargain book company. Another option is to gift your overstock or remainder books to a nonprofit organization.

Bargain Book Companies

Bargain book companies are a growing industry. One of the strategies CBA has been promoting to member retail stores to help them draw in customers is to have a bargain book center in the store.

Bargain book companies purchase remainders, overstocks, and damaged skids and then sell these books to retailers to sell at highly discounted prices: generally between 80-90% off the listed retail price. Of course, this means these companies buy your overstock, remainders, and damaged skids for pennies per book.

Here is how it usually works. You submit a copy of the title that you want to liquidate to a bargain book company with information on how many you have available for them to purchase. The company then gives you an offer on the books. You can choose to accept or reject the offer. If you accept the offer, the bargain book company pays you cash on delivery of your books (they also pay for the shipping). When selling books to a remainder company, it is wise to mark the books with a small black mark (usually near the price). This way, a store cannot return the book to you or your wholesale company as a "return" for credit against their account.

Below are bargain book companies that sell to the Christian retail marketplace. If you need to liquidate overstock or damaged skids for books that you are still actively selling in the Christian retail market, you may want to choose a bargain book company that sells to the secular marketplace as most retail stores will not stock your title at normal price and also have it in the bargain book center. With some bargain book companies you can specify which particular stores you do not want your book sold to so that there is no cross-over from your sales and the bargain book company's greatly reduced cost of your book to the Christian retail marketplace.

- **Bible Factory Outlet**

    This discount chain has 55 stores around the country. They purchase overstocks and remainders and then sell these Christian materials in their stores.

Bible Factory Outlet
Corp Office/Distribution Center
6325 US Hwy 431 South
Albertville, AL 35950
888-422-4253
www.bibleoutlet.com

- **Good Steward Books**

  This company specializes in discount Christian books, Bibles, and more. They are a family business and sell primarily to the Christian marketplace.

  Good Steward Books
  9619 State Route 38
  Milford Center, OH 43045
  937-349-6677
  www.goodstewardbooks.com

- **SAS & Associates**

  SAS & Associates is a Christian discount book company selling primarily to the Christian retail marketplace. They are the nation's largest redistributor of Christian bargain books.

  SAS & Associates
  2212 Mohawk Ave.
  Knoxville, TN 37915
  865-544-5707
  www.sasdcb.com

- **Bargain Books Wholesale**

  Bargain Books Wholesale sells to both the secular and the Christian retail marketplace.

Bargain Books Wholesale
3030 29th St. SE
Grand Rapids, MI 49512
616-949-1324
www.bargainbookswholesale.com

- **Kudzu Book Traders**

    This company sells more heavily to the secular marketplace but does some sales to the Christian retail marketplace.

    Kudzu Book Traders
    200 Cook St.
    Cartersville, GA 30120
    800-262-7587
    www.kudzubooktraders.com

A fairly comprehensive list of major bargain book distributors can be found online at **www.springbookshow.com**. This is the website for the Spring Book Show, one of the premier bargain book shows in the nation. The website hosts a list of bargain book distributors who exhibit at the show.

Gifting Books to a Nonprofit Organization

There are a number of nonprofit organizations designed to receive and redistribute larger amounts of books to needy individuals for great causes. These organizations welcome boxes of overstock or remainder titles. When you choose to gift books to a nonprofit organization, you do not get money for your books, but you can usually claim a tax deduction for books donated to a qualified 501(c)(3) nonprofit organization.

Here are some non-propfits that accept bulk book donations.

- **World Vision**

    World Vision is a Christian relief and development organization operating in 100 countries around the world including the United States. They are dedicated to helping children and their communities worldwide reach their full potential by tackling the causes of poverty. With World Vision you can select which countries you want your books distributed to.

    World Vision
    Gifts-In-Kind Department
    412-749-1800
    www.worldvision.org/gik

- **Christian Resources International**

    This nonprofit organization provides free Christian literature to needy Christians throughout the world. They ship Bibles, books, Sunday school materials, tracts, and more to missionaries and pastors to equip them in their ministry.

    Christian Resources International
    P.O. Box 356 / 200 Free Street
    Fowlerville, MI 48836
    1-888-CRI-WORD
    http://cribooks.homestead.com

- **The Library of Hope**

    This ministry supports prison chaplains. It is part of Operation Starting Line, an alliance of Prison Fellowship, Billy Graham Evangelistic Association, Promise Keepers, Campus Crusade for Christ, and about 25 other ministries.

Their goal is to bring the Good News to every prisoner in America. One of the ways they strive to meet their goal is by giving Christian books and other resources to prisoners.

The Library of Hope
3020 N. El Paso St., Suite 102
Colorado Springs, CO 80907
719-632-3880
http://libraryofhope.org

• **National Association for the Exchange of Industrial Resources (NAEIR)**
This nonprofit association solicits donations of valuable, new merchandise from American companies and redistributes it to nonprofit organizations, churches, and schools to be used solely for the care of the ill, the needy, and minors.

NAEIR
560 McClure St.
Galesburg, IL 61401
800-562-0955
donor@naeir.org
www.naeir.org

Summary

Whether you choose to sell your remainder and overstock books to a bargain bookseller or gift them to a charity, your books can still have the impact of touching someone's life for eternal purposes. Even business disappointments can turn into spiritual successes through these means.

Section III

Special Markets

The Christian Homeschool Market 11

*Train a child in the way he should go,
and when he is old he will not turn from it.*

—*Proverbs 22:6*

HOMESCHOOLING IS A GROWING phenomenon. The Home School Legal Defense Association (HSLDA) estimates that homeschooling is growing from 7-15% each year with up to two million children currently homeschooled in the United States. While it is difficult to come by a number citing how many of these homeschoolers are "Christian," it is generally believed that Christians make up the majority of the homeschool market (up to 72%). This growth in homeschooling has spurred an estimated $750 million annual market supplying parents with teaching materials and lesson aids. The National Center for Education Statistics (NCES) reports that the average homeschool family spends $600 per child per year on educational resources.

Even if your book is not specifically geared toward homeschoolers but lends itself to this market, consider including this growing group in your marketing plans and efforts. As with any product, the key to selling in the homeschool market is gaining the attention of your target audience. A growing number of avenues are available to promote and sell your products in the Christian homeschool marketplace.

Distribution to Christian Retail Stores

With the growth of homeschooling, CBA has encouraged their members to include a homeschool section in their stores. CBA sees this as one way for Christian retail stores to continually reinvent themselves to remain viable in the bookstore marketplace. While all Christian wholesale book companies are willing to carry some homeschool materials, Appalachian is the company that has positioned itself as the homeschool material source for Christian retail stores.

- **Appalachian**
    Pat Marcum, Director of Homeschooling
    522 Princeton Rd
    PO Box 1573
    Johnson City, TN 37601
    800-289-2772
    pat.marcum@stl.org
    www.appalink.com

Appalachian also hosts a website where homeschoolers can find Christian stores near them that sell Christian homeschool products. This website is www.homeschoolheadquarters.com

Homeschool Magazines

One good way to reach a large segment of the homeschooling population is through magazines for homeschoolers. These magazines offer a variety of ways for publishers and authors to promote their products.

Purchasing advertising in homeschool magazines is one way to place your product before homeschoolers on a regular basis. Another is to write articles for these magazines. Writing articles for or placing excerpts from your latest titles in homeschool magazines can grab homeschoolers' attention and increase your book sales.

Homeschool magazines also provide product reviews for their readers. Some accept products directly and generate their own reviews while others only accept review articles from homeschoolers who have used a product and approve of it. Many of the homeschool magazines post their product reviews on their websites and feature them in their e-zines along with publishing the reviews in their print magazine.

Homeschool families rely on these reviews when considering new or supplementary material to buy for their individual homeschool programs. Unlike most publications that provide reviews, many homeschooling magazines do not require that a product be brand new. As long as a product is newer or new to the homeschool market, these publications are willing to consider reviewing the product.

As with any review, it is best to contact the editor of each publication before submitting your products. This allows editors to provide information and instructions on how they want products submitted and keeps you, the publisher, from wasting time and money sending out materials to magazines that will not review your book.

Following are six main national publications that reach the Christian homeschool market:

- *Homeschooling Today*
  P.O. Box 436
  Barker, TX 77413
  281-492-6050
  editor@homeschooltoday.com
  www.homeschooltoday.com

- *Homeschool Enrichment Magazine*
  Homeschool Enrichment, Inc.
  P.O. Box 163
  Pekin, IL 61555
  800-558-9523
  editor@homeschoolenrichment.com
  www.homeschoolenrichment.com

- *Practical Homeschooling*
  Home Life, Inc.
  Mary Pride
  1731 Smizer Mill Rd.
  Fenton, MO 63026
  636-343-6786
  news@home-school.com
  www.home-school.com

- *TEACH Magazine*
  Lorrie Flem
  18016 West Spring Lake Drive
  Renton, WA 98058
  Lorrie@TEACHmagazine.com
  www.TEACHmagazine.com

- *The Homeschool Digest*
    Wisdom's Gate
    Skeet Savage, Editor
    P.O. Box 374
    Covert, MI 49043
    editor@wisgate.com
    www.homeschooldigest.com

- *The Old Schoolhouse Magazine*
    Kate Kessler
    Products Review Manager
    P.O. Box 185
    Cool, CA 95614
    530-823-0447
    kate-kessler@thehomeschoolmagazine.com
    www.thehomeschoolmagazine.com

Christian Homeschool Websites

Many homeschool families seek support through the Internet. As a result, a fair number of Christian homeschool support websites exist. These sites function as multi-purpose places which feature information, chat rooms, message boards, helpful links, and reviews of products. Many also sell homeschool products on their website.

Homeschool support websites offer many opportunities for publishers and authors to promote books to Christian homeschoolers. Publishers and authors can submit books to these websites for review, join the discussion groups, write articles for either the website or its e-newsletter, advertise on the website or in the site's e-newsletter, and become an affiliate. Some of these support websites receive over 4,000 visitors a day.

A few of the larger Christian homeschooling websites are listed here.

- **HomeschoolChristian.com**
  www.homeschoolchristian.com
  Mary Leggewie, Owner
  mary@homeschoolchristian.com
  Martha Robinson, Product Reviews
  MRobinson@HomeschoolChristian.com

- **Eclectic Homeschool**
  www.eho.org
  Beverly Krueger, Publisher
  Editor@eho.org
  For article submissions
  articles@eho.org
  Tammy Cardwell, Product Reviews
  tammyc@eho.org

- **Homeschooling From the Heart**
  www.homeschoolingfromtheheart.com
  Cindy Prechtel
  Homeschool Reviews For You
  1241 Wendell Avenue
  North Fort Myers, FL 33903
  newsletter@homeschoolingfromtheheart.com

- **Home School Blessings**
  www.homeschoolblessings.com
  734-718-8939
  Byron, MI 48418

- **Home Educators Resource Directory**
    This website provides comprehensive resources for the general and Christian homeschool market.
    www.homeeddirectory.com
    1102 E. Las Palmaritas Drive
    Phoenix, AZ 85020
    602-413-4814
    info@homeeddirectory.com

- **National African-American Homeschoolers Alliance (NAAHA)**
    This is a nonsectarian website for African-American families who homeschool.
    www.naaha.com
    info@naaha.com

Homeschool Mail-Order Catalogs

Many homeschool families order from homeschool catalogs when purchasing materials for their homeschool program. Numerous homeschool catalogs are available in the Christian homeschool market. Many publishers of homeschool materials produce catalogs showcasing their products and include products from other publishers.

Placement of your book in a Christian homeschool catalog helps increase exposure for your title in this growing marketplace. Each catalog company has its own review process for considering materials for inclusion in its product catalog. Make sure that you contact each catalog company to acquire their submission guidelines and to ensure that they are currently accepting materials prior to submitting materials for inclusion.

A few of the larger Christian homeschool catalogs are mentioned here.

- **Christian Book Distributors (CBD)**
    Homeschool Catalog
    Stephen Tiller
    140 Summit Street
    Peabody, MA 01960
    www.christianbook.com

- **Appalachian**
    Pat Marcum, Director of Homeschooling
    522 Princeton Rd.
    PO Box 1573
    Johnson City, TN 37601
    pat.marcum@stl.org
    www.appalink.com

- **Sonlight Catalog**
    Sonlight Curriculum, Ltd.
    8042 South Grant Way
    Littleton, CO 80122
    303-730-6292
    www.sonlight.com

- **Love to Learn**
    741 North State Rd. 198
    Salem, UT 84653
    888-771-1034
    www.lovetolearn.net

- **Books on the Path**
    PO Box 436
    Barker, TX 77413
    www.booksonthepath.com

- **Timberdoodle Company**
    1510 E Spencer Lake Rd.
    Shelton, WA 98584
    360-426-0672
    mailbag@timberdoodle.com
    www.timberdoodle.com

- **Rainbow Resource Center**
    Rt. 1 Box 159A
    50 N 500 East Rd.
    Toulon, IL 61483
    888-841-3456
    info@rainbowresource.com
    http://rainbowresource.com

- **Children's Books**
    P.O. Box 239
    Greer, SC 29652
    864-968-0391
    www.childrens-books.us

- **Queen Homeschool Supply**
    168 Plantz Ridge Rd.
    New Freeport, PA 15352
    888-695-2777
    www.queenhomeschool.com

Homeschool Conventions

A few hundred homeschool conventions are held across the United States each year. Homeschool conventions provide publishers of homeschool materials a good venue for placing your products in front of homeschoolers. Homeschool conventions feature seminars for homeschool parents to acquire new and innovative ideas for teaching their children. They also include exhibit halls with homeschool materials for attendees to browse and purchase. Most conferences produce handouts for attendees which contain some advertising of homeschool products.

Publishers who want to include speaking and exhibiting at homeschool conventions as part of a marketing plan for your products should consider joining the Homeschool Speakers and Vendors Association (HSVA). HSVA provides its members with unlimited access to a complete database of homeschool conventions. They also host a Convention Speakers Bureau which lists individuals who provide presentations at homeschool conventions. Homeschool convention planners can browse this list to find speakers for their upcoming conventions.

- **Homeschool Speakers and Vendors Association (HSVA)**
  706 Locust Pointe Place
  Louisville, KY 40245
  502-244-2843
  subscriptions@homeschoolvendors.org
  www.homeschoolvendors.org

Another source online for a listing of homeschool conventions is provided by *Homeschooling Today* on their website. This list can be found at http://homeschooltoday.com/resources/events/listallevents.php.

An affordable alternative to exhibiting materials at homeschool conventions is to participate in a convention bag stuffing program. Homeschool conventions generally provide attendees bags filled with promotional materials for homeschool products. Publishers can place marketing materials in homeschool convention attendee bags as an alternative or in addition to exhibiting at a convention. The homeschool convention market has a convention bag stuffing service run by Great Stuff Convention Bags, Inc. This service provides convention bags for over 150 homeschool conventions each year, providing more than 100,000 bags to conference attendees. Publishers can choose the conventions at which they want to make their materials available. Great Stuff Convention Bags then places your promotional materials in convention bags for a fee and delivers them to the homeschool conventions.

- **Great Stuff Convention Bags, Inc.**
    P.O. Box 7271
    Newark, DE 19714
    302-737-3673
    info@greatstuffconventionbags.com
    www.greatstuffconventionbags.com

One company has started an online homeschool convention. This convention has all the features of a physical homeschool convention, but everything is provided online. Specializing in reaching rural families, missionary families in foreign countries, and those who cannot attend a regular homeschool convention, this website provides seminars and a vendor hall available 24 hours a day, seven days a week, worldwide. For a yearly fee, publishers can be listed as a vendor on this site and maintain their own booth. Only accepted vendors are used as conference speakers on the website.

- **Homeschool Convention.com**
  Great Products
  3611 South Underbrush
  Pahrump, NV 89048
  727-403-2772
  info@homeschoolconvention.com
  www.homeschoolconvention.com

Homeschool Card Packs

Card packs offer an affordable marketing strategy in reaching the Christian homeschool market. Card packs are stacks of promotional cards from a variety of vendors bundled together in a plastic wrap package and mailed to a list of target consumers. This type of direct mail advertising is more cost effective than solo direct mail. Most card pack companies provide some design services for your post card insert promoting your products. Some companies have narrow restrictions on the size of the inserts for their card pack while others allow a wider variety on the size of the insert mailed in their card pack.

Two main companies provide card packs for the Christian homeschool market.

- **Tri-Media Marketing Services**
  Christian Family Homeschool Shopper
  6152 Overton Ridge Blvd.
  Fort Worth, TX 76132
  800-874-4062
  amyr@trimediaonline.com
  www.trimediaonline.com

- **National Response Marketing, Inc.**
    Christian Homeschool Connection
    6701 W. 64th Street, Ste. 225
    Shawnee Mission, KS 66202
    888-777-6032
    info@nrm-inc.com
    www.nrm-inc.com

Homeschool Associations

Important issues for families who homeschool are support, encouragement, and the protected right to freely home educate children. Every state hosts at least one homeschool association that works to protect the right to home educate and helps homeschool families network with each other for support. Some states have multiple associations. Homeschool associations generally provide their members with a regular newsletter. Publishers can utilize homeschool associations' newsletters to reach homeschoolers with your products. Some homeschool associations allow advertising in their newsletters while others allow article submissions featuring an author byline through which products can be promoted.

Homeschooling Today provides a comprehensive list of homeschool associations by state on their website with a link to each organization's website. This list can be found online at http://homeschooltoday.com/resources/organizations.

Homeschool e-Newsletters

A number of publishers who produce materials for the Christian homeschool market produce e-newsletters. e-Newsletters provide these publishers a way to regularly connect with previous and potential customers. Each newsletter provides the consumer with valuable information and directs them back to the publisher's products. Many publishers send their e-newsletter automatically to anyone who purchases a product and include a way for visitors to sign up for the free e-newsletter on their website.

Producing an e-newsletter can be time consuming and building a consumer base to send your newsletter to takes time. If you are a publisher with only one or two titles for the homeschool marketplace, consider piggybacking on existing e-newsletters geared toward homeschoolers to advertise your products. Many e-newsletters include paid advertisements and some will include articles from authors looking to promote their products.

While no central registry of homeschool e-newsletters exists, one good place to start is with the national homeschool magazines. Many of these offer free e-newsletters to their subscribers and to potential subscribers.

One example of this is *The Old Schoolhouse Magazine* (TOS). This magazine provides eleven different monthly e-newsletters for the Christian homeschool community. A list of such e-newsletters can be found at http://www.theoldhomeschoolhouse.com under "e-newsletter." Sarah White is the senior editor for TOS's e-newsletters and she can be reached at sarah@thehomeschoolmagazine.com.

A number of publishers publishing curriculum and materials for the Christian homeschool market produce e-newsletters with substantial circulations. Unit Study Helps produces a weekly e-newsletter that sells sponsorships (advertisements). This e-newsletter, *The Homeschoolers Notebook*, is provided weekly to over 18,000 subscribers. Unit Study Helps can be found online at www.unitstudyhelps.com. The Teaching Home produced a magazine for years. Recently they took a hiatus from the print magazine but continued to provide information through their free e-newsletter.

The Teaching Home's free e-newsletter also has a large circulation. They can be found online at www.teachinghome.com.

A new website, www.homeschoolingarticles.com, was recently launched to provide quality content for homeschool e-newsletters, e-zines, and blogs. Authors can submit articles on homeschooling topics to the website and publishers of homeschool Internet publications can use the articles posted on this website in their periodicals for free.

Homeschool Blogs

Blogs are another means to reach large numbers of homeschoolers. As a publisher or author, you can create your own homeschool blog and you can advertise on others' homeschool blogs to increase exposure of your products within the homeschool community. As blogging continues to grow in popularity, the number of homeschool blogs also grows. The largest homeschool blogging site on the Internet is www.homeschoolblogger.com, owned by *The Old Schoolhouse Magazine*. Created in 2005, this site has rapidly become the largest homeschool blogging site on the Internet with over 120 homeschool blogs. The site offers free blog sites to homeschoolers, speakers, and authors.

One idea for attracting new traffic to your blog and subsequently your website is to be part of a blog carnival. A blog carnival puts a variety of related blogs on display for blog readers to view. This exposes blog readers to new blogs on their topic of interest allowing them to find new blogs without having to do much searching. One homeschool website featuring a homeschool blog carnival is http://whyhomeschool.blogspot.com.

Homeschool eBooks

Many homeschoolers are technologically savvy and purchase ebooks for curriculum or supplemental material. For those publishers producing ebooks for the Christian homeschool market, consider finding affiliate homeschool websites to promote your ebooks. In addition to selling ebooks on your website, offer your ebooks through general market ebook stores and ebook stores geared toward the homeschool marketplace. Generally, ebook stores will list your ebook for free and pay you a percentage of each sale. One good ebook store for the homeschooling community is Homeschoolestore.com.

- **Homeschoolestore.com**
  Staley Krause, Director of Marketing
  HomeschoolEStore.com
  1609 W. Callender Ave.
  Peoria, IL 61606
  309-453-4903
  staley@homeschoolestore.com
  www.homeschoolestore.com

Creative Marketing

One self-publisher producing materials for Christian homeschoolers created a WebRing to increase Christian homeschool publishers' exposure on the Internet. This ring is designed to create a network of companies and families who self-publish Christian homeschool curriculum or supplementary materials. You can find this WebRing at http://r.webring.com/hub?ring=homeschoolcurric.

Summary

As the homeschool market continues to grow, the need for quality materials for this group will continue to increase. The opportunities for marketing in this growing marketplace are increasing and changing each year.

eBooks 12

He put a new song in my mouth, a hymn of praise to our God.
Many will see and fear and put their trust in the Lord.
—Psalm 40:3

THE eBOOK INDUSTRY IS BLOOMING. According to Dan Rose, director of digital media for Amazon.com, ebooks account for about one-tenth of one percent of the books sold in the United States. While still a small percentage of the overall publishing industry, around two million ebooks were sold in 2005 making ebooks a multi-million dollar industry.

Traditional publishers are getting onboard with ebooks, making many of their print bestsellers also available as ebooks. Currently, the bestselling ebooks are bestseller print books that have been made available in ebook format. As ebooks have become more popular, public libraries have begun to purchase ebooks and make them available for their patrons to borrow a download.

Traditionally, the Christian marketplace has lagged behind the trends in the general marketplace. This appears to be holding true for ebooks. At this time, the Christian marketplace has not yet embraced ebooks. This marketplace is only now beginning to foresee the market shift toward and the earning potential in ebooks. *Publishers Weekly* reported that Thomas Nelson, a large Christian publishing house, recently issued a statement that they were planning to join the ebook market and were preparing for digital sales, even though the market wasn't there yet. Zondervan®, however, is already selling some ebook versions of their print titles on their website. Web stores, review sources, and marketing channels specifically for Christian ebooks have yet to be developed as the Christian marketplace is not yet fully onboard with ebooks.

Publishers and authors who are developing Christian-themed ebooks must, at this time, utilize general market ebook web stores and marketing channels to promote and sell your ebooks. Most of the resources listed in this chapter will be general market resources that also feature some religious materials.

Staying Informed

eBook technology is rapidly progressing and changing. Publishers of ebooks must stay abreast of this technology to remain viable in the ebook market.

eBook publishers can stay informed about ebook news and technology through subscribing to free e-zines dedicated to these issues. One such e-zine is *eBooks N' Bytes Informer* which can be found online at **www.ebooksnbytes.com**.

Joining an online discussion group for ebook publishers provides another way to stay informed about the industry and what other e-publishers are doing. Two e-publisher discussion groups are eBook Talk at **www.ebooknews.netfirms.com** and Ind-e-Pubs at **www.ind-e-pubs.com**.

For ebook authors, Christian Electronic Authors provides an online forum for discussing electronic publishing and inspirational writing for electronic books. The group can be found online at http://groups.yahoo.com/group/Christian-e-author. Additionally, Christian Electronic Authors' website at www.christianeauthor.com is a good resource for ebook authors. This site features announcements of new ebook releases, author interviews, and links to author websites.

Digital Publishing Trade Associations

eBook publishers and authors can belong to any traditional publishers or authors association and receive great information, benefits, and networking opportunities. However, there are a couple general market trade associations specifically geared toward ebook authors and publishers.

- **The International Digital Publishing Forum (IDPF)**
  IDPF is a trade and standards organization dedicated to the development and promotion of electronic publishing. The IDPF welcomes book, magazine, journal, and newspaper publishers producing materials in the digital reading format to join the organization.
  www.idpf.org

- **Electronically Published Internet Connection (EPIC)**
  EPIC is geared toward published authors who have a book in ebook format. Publishers can also join this organization.
  www.epicauthors.org

eBook Reviews

Few Christian publications or Christian book review websites are currently providing reviews of ebooks. However, as the movement toward ebooks continues, more online review sites will begin to add ebook reviews as the Christian marketplace gets onboard with this trend. Most of the reviewers listed here provide submission guidelines on their websites.

- **Christian Reviews**
  - http://come.to/bookreviews#
  - www.dancingword.net/bookreviews.htm

- **Blogs That Provide Reviews of Christian eBooks**
  - www.ebookreader.blogspot.com
  - http://catholicbooks.blogspot.com

Websites providing ebook reviews for the general market commonly feature at least one religious book category as each of the websites listed below do.

- **eBook-Only Reviews for General Market**
  - www.ebook-reviews.net
  - www.knowbetter.com
  - www.geocities.com/ebook_review

- **General Market Reviews Including eBook Reviews**
  - www.bookreview.com
  - www.review-books.com
  - www.myshelf.com
  - www.compulsivereader.com
  - www.blackbookreview.com

- *ForeWord Magazine*
    ForeWord Magazine, a general market trade magazine, includes reviews of POD and ebooks from independent presses in their print magazine.
    www.forewordmagazine.com

eBook Directories

eBook directories allow you to list your ebook on a site with other ebooks. Listing in ebook directories allows you to reach ebook readers. Some ebook directories provide free listings while others charge fees to list ebooks. Utilizing free ebook directories to advertise your ebooks only costs you the time it takes to list your book with each directory.

There are some ebook directories exclusively for free ebooks on the Internet. If you offer a free ebook download on your website to hook customers into purchasing more of your products, listing your free ebook in these directories can be a useful marketing tool. These directories will generate more traffic for your website, which can lead to more paying customers.

A few ebook directories are listed here for your reference.

- **Free Listing eBook Directories**
    - www.mindlikewater.com
    - www.wisdomebooks.com
    - www.jogena.com
    - www.ebooksnbytes.com
    - www.ebookjungle.com

- Fee Based eBook Directories
    - www.e-bookdirectory.com
    - www.knowbetter.com

- eBook Directories for Free eBooks
    - www.free-ebooks.net
    - www.ebookdirectory.com

eBook Press Release Services

Another avenue for spreading the word about your new ebooks is to utilize an online press release service. These services broadcast announcements both to publications and consumers. There are a few free ebook press release services online. Two of these are www.ebookbroadcast.com and www.prweb.com. Other websites such as www.ebooknews.netfirms.com allow you to announce an ebook on their website for free. For a fee, www.netsurf.com will list your ebook in their free e-zine, *Netsurfer Books*, which is sent to an opt-in mailing list.

Online eBook Stores

Having your ebook listed with online ebook stores can help you sell more books. There are a number of online stores focused on selling ebooks. Following is a list of some of the top online ebook stores.

- www.amazon.com
- www.ebooks.com
- www.fictionwise.com
- www.cyberread.com

- www.ereader.com
- www.fictionwise.com
- www.ebookwise.com
- www.ebookexplorer.com
- www.e-book-zone.com

Library Distribution

A number of public libraries have begun to offer their patrons ebook services. These services allow library users to borrow a download of an ebook for a specified period of time. Traditional library book distributors are currently not selling ebook services to libraries. eBook library services have stepped in to fill this demand. A few of these services are listed here.

- NetLibrary
    www.netlibrary.com

- LibWise
    www.libwise.com

- ebrary
    www.ebrary.com

eBook Awards

For the most part, traditional book awards do not offer awards for ebooks. Electronically Published Internet Connection (EPIC), an organization for ebook authors, has developed book awards for ebooks. Named the EPPIE Awards, these awards recognize outstanding achievement in electronic publishing. Awards are given

in twenty different ebook categories. More information on the EPPIE Awards can be found on EPIC's website.
www.epicauthors.org/eppies.html

Creative Marketing

As the trend toward more digital technology continues, publishers and authors of print books should consider the ebook market as a means to broaden your exposure and sales. Your published print books can be offered in ebook format also, bringing you sales from those individuals who prefer to read in digital format. You can increase your sales and website traffic by offering a free ebook on your website. This free ebook can be a book you are no longer offering in print format or it might be a novella or short story by one of your authors to whet the appetite of e-readers prompting them to come back and purchase that author's other titles. For those unsure where and how to start implementing an ebook download on your website, services such as PayLoadz at **www.payloadz.com** are available. PayLoadz provides digital goods e-commerce services for websites selling intangible goods online.

Spanish Language Books 13

After this I looked and there before me was a great multitude that no one could count, from every nation, tribe, people, and language, standing before the throne and in front of the Lamb.
—Revelation 7:9

HISPANICS ARE THE LARGEST and fastest-growing minority group in the United States. The most recent census shows this group accounts for one out of every eight U.S. residents. Hispanic population growth is no longer exclusively concentrated in the Southern states. Midwestern states such as Iowa and Indiana are beginning to see dramatic growth rates of this population. Additionally, the average Hispanic family income is increasing, making this population an ever more viable consumer.

Along with the population increase, Spanish language products are growing and selling well in the United States. Editorial Unilit, a publisher of Spanish language materials, makes 70% of its sales in the United States and 30% overseas. Ten years ago those figures were reversed.

Some estimates place the sales increase of Spanish language Christian titles as high as 30% per year for the past couple years. Interestingly, the Spanish titles that are the biggest sellers in the

Hispanic Christian book market are almost all translations of English language books.

In 2003, the Association of American Publishers (AAP) named June Latino Book Month to promote books for and by Latinos. Since that time, tradeshows and book fairs for this language group have increased dramatically.

Spanish Language Products Association

As a result of the growth of Spanish language Christian products, many large Christian publishing houses have added Spanish language divisions. The Spanish Evangelical Products Association (SEPA), a publishers association, was formed to serve the growing number of Christian publishers producing Spanish language materials. SEPA encourages Christian retailers to reach out to the Hispanic market. They recently published a free "Ten Steps to Reaching the Hispanic Market" guide for retailers, which includes a listing of Spanish Evangelical publishers and distributors.

- Spanish Evangelical Products Association (SEPA)
  1370 NW 88 Ave.
  Miami, FL 33172
  305-503-1195
  sepa@bsmi.com
  www.sepalit.com

Spanish Language Tradeshows

Spanish Christian product shows are increasing in number in the United States as well as in Mexico and Central America. These annual tradeshows present an opportunity for publishers to display

Spanish language titles to the Christian Spanish-speaking retail marketplace.

- **Expolit**

    This Hispanic Christian products tradeshow is held in Florida, the Caribbean, and Central America.
    www.expolit.com

- **Expo Cristiana**

    This Spanish language Christian products tradeshow is held annually in Mexico City, Mexico.
    www.expocristiana.com

- **Latino Book and Family Festival**

    Hosted by Latino Literacy Now, this festival is a traveling book show for the general Hispanic market. Each year they hold festivals in Houston, Dallas, Los Angeles, and Chicago. These festivals feature exhibitors and speakers.
    www.lbff.us

Spanish Language Book Reviews

There are a few Christian Spanish language publications in the United States providing reviews of Spanish language books. One such publication is:

- *Revista Enfoque*

    This Spanish language Christian magazine published by Expolit Promotions, a division of Expolit, is distributed to Spanish-speaking Christian readers in North America, Latin

America, and the Caribbean. The magazine features book reviews and advertisements.
www.revistaenfoque.com

Additionally, many industry trade publications are now providing reviews of Spanish language books either in each edition of their magazine or just in special Spanish language editions.

- *Christian Retailing*

This magazine for Christian retailers now has a section of each edition devoted to news and reviews of Spanish language titles.

Contact:
- Harold Goerzen at hgoerzen@hcjb.org or 719-388-2264

www.christianretailing.com

- *Christian Library Journal*

This online journal providing reviews of Christian material for church and Christian school librarians currently devotes one issue each year to Spanish language titles.

Nancy Hesch, Editor
Church Library Services
1225 Johnson St.
Wenatchee, WA 98801
509-662-7455
nlhesch@christianlibraryj.org
www.christianlibraryj.org

- *Library Journal*

    This adult book review journal for public and academic librarians provides regular reviews of Spanish language materials that fit their review criteria.

    Criticas
    Attn: Carmen Ospina
    Library Journal
    360 Park Avenue South
    New York, New York 10010
    www.libraryjournal.com

Spanish Language Distribution

The major Christian book distributors and wholesale book companies (see Chapter 2) all stock and sell Spanish language titles as many Christian retail stores are now beginning to include a Spanish language section as part of their store offerings. However, reaching the Christian Spanish-language-only stores takes a little more effort. There are a few Christian distributors who focus solely on selling books to Spanish language bookstores.

- **Spanish Speaking Bookstore Distributions**

    This company is the largest distributor in the United States of Catholic and Protestant Spanish language religious materials. Their focus is bookstores, seminaries, and direct orders.
    www.spanishbookstore.com

- **Pan De Vida Distributors**
    www.pandevida.com

- Visión Joven
    www.visionjoven.com

- Distrilibros, Inc.
    Inter-American Book Distributors
    www.distrilibros.com

Increasingly large-box retailers such as Wal-Mart®, Costco®, and Sam's Club® are selling Spanish language products including Christian Spanish language products. A few distributors for these large-box retailers now specialize in Spanish language books.

The following are some distributors who specialize in the distribution of Spanish language books to these large general market retailers.

- Anderson Merchandisers
    This company sells to Wal-Mart.
    www.amerch.com

- Levy Home Entertainment
    Levy sells to Target, Wal-Mart, Kmart™, and Toys R Us®.
    www.levybooks.com

- Advanced Marketing Services (AMS)
    AMS sells to Costco and Sam's Club.
    www.advmkt.com

Spanish Language Marketing

As Spanish language Christian books increase, so must the marketing avenues for these books. A few companies produce catalogs for bookstores to use to reach their Spanish-speaking Christian customers.

- **Expolit Catalog**

    Expolit Promotions, a division of the Expolit convention, produces a product catalog that reaches over 100,000 Spanish-speaking consumers in the United States and Latin America.
    info@expolit.com
    www.expolit.com

- **Munce Group**

    Munce is now producing a Spanish language catalog, in addition to their regular English catalogs, that their member stores can purchase and mail to consumers.
    sue.brewer@munce.com
    www.munce.com

Spanish Radio and Television

Authors seeking to be media guests on Spanish radio and television must speak fluent Spanish (unless you are being interviewed for an English station that also broadcasts in Spanish) as Christian Spanish radio and television stations are aired in Spanish. Many Spanish radio and television stations broadcast to Central and South America as well as North America. When looking to find Spanish stations to query for guest appearances a few options are available for authors and publishers.

- **Radio-Locator**

    This website features a radio station search engine that includes Spanish language radio stations in the United States

as well as worldwide radio stations.
www.radio-locator.com

- **Christian Television Network International (CTN)**
    CTN is broadcast out of Florida to the United States, Canada, Central and South America, and parts of Europe.
    www.ctni.org

- **Club 700 Hoy**
    Club 700 Hoy is a Spanish 700 Club program.
    www.club700hoy.com

- **Catholic Radio and Television Network (CRTN)**
    This network provides a listing of Catholic radio stations in North and South America including Spanish language radio stations with links to each station's website.
    www.crtn.org/radio

Authors and publishers can also use a press release service to target Hispanic radio, television, and other media outlets to gain exposure for their books. Companies that offer Hispanic newswire services are geared toward the general Hispanic marketplace, but often include Christian Spanish language media contacts.

- **Hispanic Newswire**
    This service, offered by PR Newswire, offers comprehensive distribution to Spanish language media in the United States. Releases are distributed to newspapers, magazines, television and radio media, and websites.
    www.prnewswire.com

Spanish Language Book Awards

Currently, the only Christian Spanish language book awards are given by SEPA (Spanish Evangelical Products Association). Since almost all of the bestselling Spanish language Christian titles are translated versions of bestselling English language Christian books, many of the awards given by SEPA generally mirror ECPA's Christian Book Awards.

- **Spanish Evangelical Products Association (SEPA) Book Awards**
  These awards include the Harold Kregel Book of the Year Award, the Best Original Spanish Work of the Year Award, and Gallery of Honor Silver, Gold, and Platinum Awards based on sales figures for a title.

There are a few Spanish language book awards for the general book marketplace. One such award program has been implemented by Latino Literacy Now. While this program is not specifically geared toward Christian books, religious books can be submitted for consideration in the award categories offered.

- **International Latino Book Awards**
  These awards accept nominated titles from South, Central, and North America. Awards are given for children/youth, fiction, and nonfiction categories and are presented each year at BookExpo America.
  www.lbff.us

Summary

For those publishers with existing Spanish language books and for those considering translating their current titles into Spanish, the good news is the market for Spanish language Christian titles is expanding and it will continue to grow as the Hispanic population continues to increase in the United States.